# A. D. SALISBURY

# Death, and memory.

*Copyright © 2024 by A. D. Salisbury*

*All rights reserved. No part of this publication may be reproduced, stored or transmitted in any form or by any means, electronic, mechanical, photocopying, recording, scanning, or otherwise without written permission from the publisher. It is illegal to copy this book, post it to a website, or distribute it by any other means without permission.*

*A. D. Salisbury asserts the moral right to be identified as the author of this work.*

*A. D. Salisbury has no responsibility for the persistence or accuracy of URLs for external or third-party Internet Websites referred to in this publication and does not guarantee that any content on such Websites is, or will remain, accurate or appropriate.*

*Designations used by companies to distinguish their products are often claimed as trademarks. All brand names and product names used in this book and on its cover are trade names, service marks, trademarks and registered trademarks of their respective owners. The publishers and the book are not associated with any product or vendor mentioned in this book. None of the companies referenced within the book have endorsed the book.*

*First edition*

*Illustration by D. North*
*Cover art by D. North*

*This book was professionally typeset on Reedsy.*
*Find out more at reedsy.com*

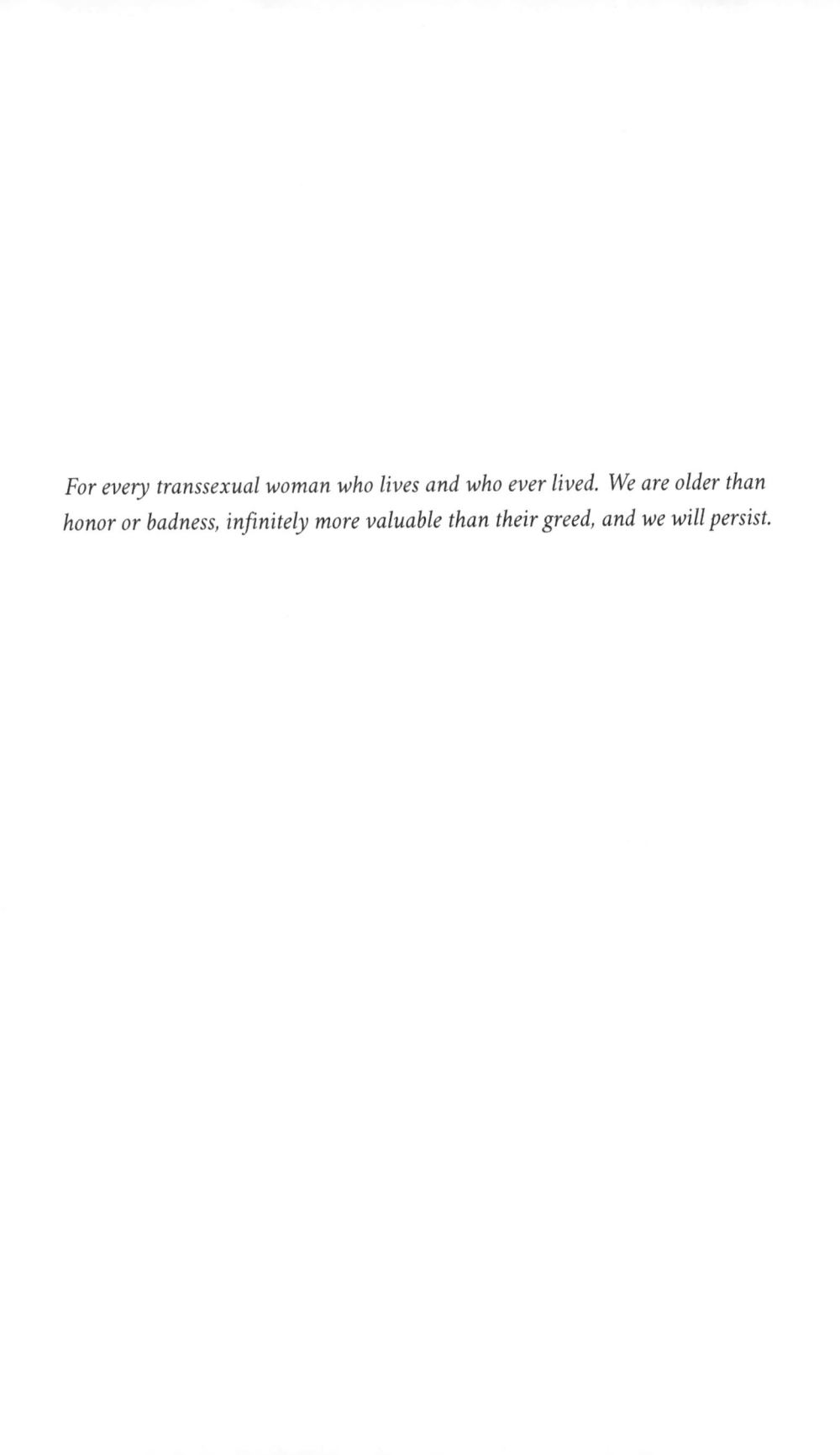

*For every transsexual woman who lives and who ever lived. We are older than honor or badness, infinitely more valuable than their greed, and we will persist.*

# Contents

*Preface* ii

## I  Essays

1. Namesake. — 3
2. Build it from ashes… — 4
3. 41% — 8
4. Make your decision. — 13
5. Defining fascism. — 16
6. The threat of free will. — 25
7. There are ten stages of genocide. — 34
8. It didn't start with stage one… — 46
9. A brief history of "experimental" medicine. — 57
10. The Chair Paradox — 64
11. Whiteness is hegemonic. — 71
12. Transmisogyny is the economy. — 76
13. Heterosexuality: The Economic Regime. — 84
14. Editorial Interferences — 95

## II  More Essays!

15. Transgender Joy and Despair (Amethysta Herrick) — 101
16. Be Queer, Do Heresy (Evelyne Rideout) — 102
17. Solidarity, til my last breath. (Kerry Garnick) — 110

*Sources/References* 112

# Preface

Part 1 of this book is a collection of essays written by the author. Part 2 is a collection of essays written by friends of the author who are also trans women. Her hope is that readers will engage critically with the world around them based on these writings.

We are living in a time of escalating fascism. Fascists across the world are consolidating power. As it was in Nazi Germany, there are many echoes today. The Nazis targeted trans people before they targeted the Jews. Today, modern fascists of all identifiers are doing the same.

"History repeats itself, first as tragedy, second as farce." - Karl Marx.

The project that culminated in this book is really just one trans woman's attempt to defy history. The author, A.D. Salisbury, is facing her own extinction. She is an internal refugee within the United States, and, in 2022, was forced to flee her family, community, and connections in Utah to try and make it in Colorado because of the trends of success towards genocidal pogroms in the United States of America's so-called "red-states". A.D. knows she probably won't survive the next decade, but she's determined to try. Failing that, she wants her words to be archived in history, so that she can never truly be erased.

# I

# Essays

*These are essays written by A.D. Salisbury. Most of them cover the nature of fascism in the status-quo. They all address a piece of her story, as a trans woman navigating life in the United States.*

# 1

# Namesake.

Most trans people don't get the luxury of being seen as who we are in life, or remembered as who we were in death. Our birth names and the false identity thrust upon us are our grave- literally and figuratively. That's why we call them deadnames- because we can no longer evade them in death. The false idea of who we were is what waits for us. For cis people, they often have the legacy of families and friends who carry their memory, and sometimes even a moneyed legacy of places and programs in their name, but for us- for trans people- when we die, we will be erased forever.

Trans people have to choose to live freely, unapologetically, and fully while we can. While all humans only get one life on this planet, trans people aren't afforded the dignity of being remembered after we die. Stories and memories can keep people alive in a subtle way. The retelling of a human's life, the lessons learned, the pain felt, the joy expressed are all a way of the dead touching the living. Trans people don't get the luxury of being able to live on like that. The forces that want us dead now have also already ensure that we won't live on in memory.

# 2

# Build it from ashes…

I became alive 2.5 years ago, give or take a handful of days. By the time this is published, it'll be closer to three years. No, you aren't reading the words of a toddler. Rather, these are the screams of a queer woman who knows she is doomed to die.

Patriarchy demands manhood of me. Having failed that assignment, it now demands my discardation and death. I do not get the luxury of an average life expectancy. I do not have the comfort of people treating me normally, whatever that means. I don't even get the result of a body that reflects who I am. Thanks to gatekeeping doctors and a bipartisan consensus of "trannies evil", my transition has been gummed up at every stage. When I can no longer provide value enough to the capitalists, I will be killed. It is likely that I will be killed even before then by their social enforcers. Whether through medical malpractice or some jackboot thug on the street, the odds are ever not in my favor.

Before I came out, before I started transitioning, there are glimpses where my memories should be. I remember the pain and the pantomiming, but the rest is hazy. I can't tell this to the family who stayed without losing them, because it would mean their fears were, to a degree, correct. I am not the same as I was. I didn't exist before transition. Transitioning was asserting who I am from the ashes of a facade that could no longer maintain homeostasis. The problem with mimicking for so long is that I don't know who I am, at all, much less in the same way many people do. My body is 27 years old. As I write this, my birthday just came and went. I should be in the stride of my career and building family and doing as well as anyone can in this extractionist hellhole, but instead I am still constructing me.

All of who I am is built from the ashes of who I was supposed to be. If I ever dreamed a dream, or if I were to reclaim and possess a dream now, I have yet to figure out how to untangle expectation and mimickry from it. We are all social creatures, and none of us live in a vacuum. Yet, my social bonds were all destroyed by the radical act of declaring myself. Some have been reforged, but most are dead and will remain dead.

I used to think I wanted to be an engineer, but that dream is simultaneously an expectation forced upon "him". When I was little, it was always "he's so smart, he'll save the world". Then came the dissociation and burnout and the hells of a testosterone driven puberty.

Every detail of the life I am building is haunted by the life I was supposed to lead. Even the name I chose for myself honors the meaning and intent behind my deadname. Every decision, from what to study in college, to who I date, to what I do in my day-to-day, is influenced by a ghost. "He" isn't really a ghost, however, because that would imply "he" lived. It's such a big deal, and yet, any way I go, all I'm doing is building from the ashes of "his" dreams, or the expectations "he" faced. To stress the point, I am not him.

**Can you truly construct yourself if you don't know who or what you're constructing?**

Beyond my existential questions, of course, is the material reality that drives them. I may have a collection of skills that I salvaged from the wreck of "his" death, writing (hopefully) among them. That's all I have. Most of my college peers have a clarity of purpose and identity I've never experienced. They know what they want to do for a living, and most of them can say they knew that their whole life. Even if I were able to say the same, the whims of 2 years can't compare to the surety built from 20.

In the "before", when I pretended, I could get jobs like you wouldn't believe. I was often sitting on or turning down job offers. Now, it is much harder to get a job, and those few and far places that will hire me have every incentive to get rid of me. In this political environment, trans women are a liability. Not because we're terrible workers or inherently evil people, but because reactionaries will make problems for the employer that happens to employ us. I've lost so many jobs for bullshit, barely coded reasons that always boil down to transmisogyny.

An example: I used to have this job teaching children in after school programs, using legos to help them understand engineering concepts. I loved it, and the kids loved me. But, the schools I would go to made things harder than they needed to be. There was this one catholic school I was assigned to where the parents called my usual outfits "costumes" and the administrators would force me to use the men's restroom. That school was built so all the staff/adult restrooms were single-occupancy, which shouldn't even matter, but it means that they couldn't even argue about my presence making other women uncomfortable. My boss found out what I was dealing with and moved me to another school. Despite a supportive boss, I am no longer with that company for reasons beyond my control.

When I wrote "mimicking" earlier, I meant it. I could never connect with manhood. The best I could muster was copying men I knew and assuming their behaviors in the contexts I experienced them in. I had several male role models. My first decent boss, my grandpa, my gay uncles, and my nana's husband all taught me their way of being a man. I would copy those ways in the contexts I could in order to survive social interactions. Yet, surviving is not living.

I have learned that I can survive anything. Short of being regendered to manhood, I don't think anything will cause me to "unalive" by my own hand. However, I am eternally yearning for more than surviving. I know I won't ever be allowed to thrive, but the middle ground of "living" sounds nice. It really does. All I can do is attempt to build a life from the ashes of my own death. Maybe one day I'll experience living.

# 3

# 41%

Forces of social exclusion and social murder, through the hatred and the hostility is what leads to the claimed statistic that 41% of trans people die from suicide. It is also why we say in our community that "every trans suicide is a murder". Cis people, as a majority group, erase and minimize us in life, then bulldoze over us in death, leaving not even a speck of our real selves to be remembered once we are gone.

In terms of suicide statistics:
  - 4.0% of cis people consider suicide over their lifetimes in the US. (Substance Abuse and Mental Health Services Administration, 2016)
  - 82% of trans people consider suicide over their lifetimes. (Austin et al., 2020)
  - 40% of trans people attempt suicide over their lifetimes in the US. (Phillips, 2023)
  - 32-50% of trans people across the world attempt suicide. (Virupaksha et al., 2016)

What this data helps us illuminate is the harsh, cruel, and abusive reality trans people are subjected to every day by cis people in general and by the structures that comprise cishetero hegemony, patriarchy, and capitalism. Suicide is death by despair. In the case of trans people, that despair is always forced upon us by an unkind cis-supremacist world. Every trans person who dies from the mechanism of suicide was murdered. This isn't hyperbole or allegory, it is cold, hard, truth.

Transmisogyny is older than written language. The very first recorded transmisogynistic slur was "baeddel". That word is the reason we have the word "bad" for the concept it describes in the modern era. Both the concept of "bad" and the word itself trace their roots to "baeddel".

Sit with that for a moment- transmisogyny is arguably traceable to the modern, common conception of "good" and "bad", with culture long-constructed around otherizing trans femmes as "bad" and "evil". We aren't humans, we're baeddels. We're demons, according to "reasonable" society.

The constant noise telling queer people overall and especially trans people that we're evil, doomed to hell, sinful, even predatory for simply existing how we are is directly attributable to why some queer people embrace the symbolism and iconography of hell and damnation. Many of us see the threats and hate as the hollow fear they are. If we're all going to hell for how God, "the divine", or whatever else made us, that's just more of the same irrational exclusion we learned how to overcome from your behavior.

The fact that Christian fascism pretends to care about free will, but only values free choice if it is used in a way compatible with the Christian-fascist framework is, or should be, a damning takedown of the validity of Christianity as a social authority. In the current fascist project, which is inseparable from modern Christianity, dehumanization of trans people, especially trans women, takes many forms. One of those forms is wojaks that caricaturize trans women to using the profile photos and other photos of trans people as "gotchas" or the basis of memes on social media, and to using slurs like "tranny" "troon" "shemale" and others. Dehumanization of trans people, especially trans femmes is rampant, and constant.

There are plenty of images that are examples of often-used transphobic "wojaks". These and their variants often circulate on reactionary internet spaces. These caricatures are made with a similar contempt and with a similar purpose as the antisemitic caricatures that have pervaded history. Those spaces include message boards like 4chan. Any internet space with insufficient or unprincipled moderation, however, has the potential to become a haven of reactionary and fascist "thought", including the use and circulation of these wojaks by users.

An example of an internet space that became a haven for reactionary discourse is Twitter (now called X). After Elon Musk's acquisition of Twitter/X, the user experience crumbled. Additionally, with the Musk-led changes to Twitter's algorithm, the paid bluechecks, which are people who subscribed to Twitter Blue in order to gain a verification badge became 200% boosted in the algorithm's source code.

Prior to the Musk buyout, Twitter's verification system was used to combat fraud, scams, stolen identities, and misleading content. Additionally, pre-Musk Twitter had relatively robust content moderation which flagged and removed the most egregious examples of bigoted or vile comments at least some of the time. Under Musk, as part of the "Twitter 2.0" rollout and mass layoffs, most of Twitter's Trust & Safety moderation team was ousted.

As such, those who paid for bluechecks to skip to the front of the visibility queue were often those who held the shittiest views. They wouldn't get engagement normally, so they paid to game the algorithm. In other words, Musk's Twitter (now called "X") has become a home for Nazis and other fascists to congregate and swarm. Accounts based on dehumanizing wojaks and other images like those in the addendum have become a much bigger source of Twitter content and commentary.

The historical existence of trans women, and the hate trans women have always received is the mechanism by which modern humanity has knowledge of the concept of badness as we know it today. Trans women have been associated with evil due to prejudice and bigotry as long as we have existed. This unending hatred manifests in incredibly deep and pervasive systemic inequities. The lack of support, hatred, and artificially but deliberately enforced difficulty of our lives of trans people is why so many of us commit suicide. Being trans isn't an illness, and it doesn't come from despair or evil. Transness is joy. We are no less sacred than any other human on this planet. The true evil is in those who celebrate societal conditions that make suicide preferable to the suffering imposed on trans people for simply existing.

The social condition isn't better for trans men and mascs. They are often erased in a very different but no less evil way. The fascist project, from its sympathizers in liberals and mainstream media to its architects, thought leaders, and rank and file, doesn't generally admit that trans men exist. In the few cases where they are forced to contend with the existence of transmasculinity, members of the fascist project often reduce trans men to "confused women" or "lost lesbians". Their meaning in this framing is that transmasculine persons aren't real, and anyone who claims to be such are woman traitors who wanted to escape patriarchy. In making these claims, however, transphobes are only further reinforcing patriarchy. All transphobia is sexism and patriarchy mixed with blatant misogyny, only sometimes hiding under a few veneers of social justice language and liberal conceptions. However, the insidious way that trans men and trans masculine people are erased is just awful.

The nature of reactionary groups is that they co-opt and, eventually, dominate every space they can. If you have even a single Nazi show up at dinner, or at a bar, and that Nazi is not immediately kicked out of the space, with force if necessary, you now have a Nazi dinner, or Nazi bar. By choosing their inherently violent and genocidal beliefs, they have forfeited any decency, respect, or tolerance afforded to the rest of us as part of the social contract.

This brings us to the paradox of tolerance. Karl Popper famously described the issue.

"Unlimited tolerance must lead to the disappearance of tolerance. If we extend unlimited tolerance even to those who are intolerant, if we are not prepared to defend a tolerant society against the onslaught of the intolerant, then the tolerant will be destroyed, and tolerance with them." - Karl Popper

This is because intolerance is a force that spreads easily. Once intolerance reaches a tipping point, the tolerant are no longer tolerated. This is because intolerance becomes a norm. There is an easy solution to the paradox of tolerance, however:

We must look at tolerance as a social contract, not a moral or ethical standard. If you don't abide by the contract, you are no longer entitled to reap its benefits. In other words, bigots of any type or level of radicalization, from run-of-the-mill conservatives to outright fascists, have chosen to opt-out of the social contract involving mutual tolerance, and as such are no longer to be tolerated by civil, decent society.

The question then becomes, "Do we have a civil and decent society?" I believe nearly any working class person of at least one single additional marginalization, whether disabled, queer, trans, BIPOC, old, or young, would tell you, emphatically: "No."

This answer means it is time to address how we get to a civil, decent society. Before we can build a better society in whole, we must stop the ravages of this society, including the genocide it is currently beginning again against white queer people, the ongoing genocide of indigenous people, the eugenics of the COVID era, and the segregation and mass slavery committed to this day against black people.

# 4

# Make your decision.

I sent these words to a former friend of mine, once. I could tell that we were at the end of our friendship, and that there was nothing to be done. "I'm used to friends dropping me like a radioactive sack of shit. What's the difference if you do it too? It'll hurt, but I'm used to that particular type of pain. This is on you. Make your decision." As trans women, we don't get the luxury of friendships.

No, instead we get tenuous temporary alliances built from lead on a foundation of shifting sand. Even before the alliance is revoked, it poisons us through trauma. Just like lead, exposure to it creates mental and physical degradation that seeps into our lives and bodies for decades to follow. Friendship for trans women is much like the Romans using leaded pipes for their aqueducts. It provides connection to something necessary, but it will end in our destruction and burn us out from history.

The… every friend I've had I've known is a ticking time bomb. Eventually whatever they get from having me around is no longer worth the social consequences of associating with a trans woman. When that threshold is hit, there's rarely conversation or ceremony. The friendship is over and means of communication are cut. When they do offer me the courtesy of an explanation, it is only to monsterize me and make sure that I know that I am the problem, the monster that it isn't worth tolerating anymore.

When I sent my friend that, I already knew what her decision would be. All I could do was assert that I knew her intentions and that it wasn't going to hurt me in the way she thought. I had prepared for it, but I had been robbed of the power to try and change it. I never get to change it. Sometimes I can delay the inevitable, but only through sacrificing my dignity and offering increased domestic and errand-running labor to my friends. I have to trade favors to maintain friendship.

This is incredibly hard for me, because I've never believed in being "tit for tat" in friendship or any relationship. As a trans woman, those are the only relationships I'm allowed by the social structure. If I want friends, I have to denigrate myself and counter my own beliefs, or they'll just leave. I don't get the luxury of friendship. Trans women need comrades and accomplices, but we aren't allowed friends. How are we supposed to build the relationships to shake this system to its foundations and help usher in a better world if we're forced into isolation. We can't, and that's the point.

If this generation of trans women is to survive, we need people willing to cross the lines constructed around us. When laws are passed to make us illegal, we need people to risk crossing those lines put into place by legislation and get us out. What I mean by "trans women need accomplices" isn't that trans women are evil criminals by choice, but that we are forced into the category of "criminal" and need people willing to color across legal lines to help us. Following the law is fine, but what other option do you have when the law doesn't let you exist peacefully? If they design the law to make it so you can't follow it, then nobody should be shocked when you've become a criminal.

We will never gain accomplices until we can forge real friendships. The moral panic is too large, despite it's subsiding. The damage has been done. Cis people are constitutionally incapable of understanding. That, or they're willfully unwilling to do so. They're passing laws to make my walking down the street a sex offense. I can't piss in peace. I can't see my mom without risking extrajudicial and legal violence. If I travel to the state where she lives, my healthcare and use of public restrooms is illegal. Even without those, if an emergency were to happen, an EMT or other first responder could refuse to provide care based on "personal beliefs", and let me die in the gutter, without consequence.

When I told my friend "make your decision" I was admitting to something all trans women know. The decision is never ours. We're not allowed to choose how we live or how we die. We're going to die younger, poorer, and lonelier than our peers. Our lives, our values, our wishes and beliefs won't matter or be remembered. Our only choice is to use our voices as we die. We can choose to scream. But we can't choose not to die prematurely.

# 5

# Defining fascism.

# DEFINING FASCISM.

*"Fascism is Social"*

"Firstly, it is not true that fascism is only the fighting organisation of the bourgeoisie. Fascism is not only a military-technical category. Fascism is the bourgeoisie's fighting organisation that relies on the active support of Social-Democracy. Social-Democracy is objectively the moderate wing of fascism. There is no ground for assuming that the fighting organisation of the bourgeoisie can achieve decisive successes in battles, or in governing the country, without the active support of Social-Democracy. There is just as little ground for thinking that Social-Democracy can achieve decisive successes in battles, or in governing the country, without the active support of the fighting organisation of the bourgeoisie. These organisations do not negate, but supplement each other. They are not antipodes, they are twins. Fascism is an informal political bloc of these two chief organisations; a bloc, which arose in the circumstances of the post-war crisis of imperialism, and which is intended for combating the proletarian revolution. The bourgeoisie cannot retain power without such a bloc. It would therefore be a mistake to think that "pacifism" signifies the liquidation of fascism. In the present situation, "pacifism" is the strengthening of fascism with its moderate, Social-Democratic wing pushed into the forefront." - Joseph Stalin

From the words of the man who led the Red Army into driving back Nazi Germany, we begin to glimpse fascism is economic. However, I contest that it is not only economic. Fascism is as much a social force as it is an economic one. It is plain that social conditions have been, in recent times at least, turning ever towards division and alienation. However this social deterioration isn't organic nor is it inevitable. It is the result of worsening economic conditions for regular people. The economy is based on real resources. These are raw materials, labor power, and to some extent- existing infrastructure and technology. Labor power is the potential and actual output of the working class. Raw materials are everything from nature, ores, trees, water, and other materials.

Because regular people are a part of the working class, we should also define the working class. The working class in modern society comprises everyone who doesn't command ownership of productive instruments and/or capital. If you own a controlling share of a large enough business, you aren't working class but capitalist class. If you own a factory, or a large farm, or a lumber mill, etc.- in other words if your wealth and income is derived from control of others' labor output and production infrastructure, you aren't working class- you are a capitalist. If your wealth and/or income comes from the work you do personally, either as an individual contractor or employee, you are working class. You are a worker, in that case. The true middle class in the real economy is what Marxists call the "petit-bourgeoisie", or people whose income and/or wealth comes from a combination of their personal labor and their formal ownership of a business or productive property.

Disabled people, unemployed people, the retired, and students are all part of what's called "the reserve army of the unemployed". This reserve of potential workers that don't currently have full employment for whatever reason is used as a means to discipline those who are fully employed into not striking. The ruling capitalists use the fact that there are people who can work but can't find work, for example, as a safeguard against mass action. The existence of unemployment guarantees the possibility of scabs. Scabs are people who cross a picket line to work during a strike, and usually get paid at higher rates than the established workers who are striking would be paid otherwise. In short, the reserve army of the unemployed are a part of the working class. "Working class" isn't defined by one's labor, it's defined by the individual's relationship to the means of production.

Yet, even a cursory conversation with mainstream citizens shows us that a ton, maybe even a majority of typical, working-class people in the USA consider themselves capitalists. They are sympathetic to capitalism to a point of supporting it. This despite their class interest being opposed to those who are the true capitalists. Capitalism generates wealth through extraction. This extraction requires, among other things, a downward trend in wages and in living conditions for the working class relative to the actual value generated by labor and the average of possible best living conditions. We can see this in real life pretty simply.

The innovation of the information age unlocked previously impossible levels of productivity. Increased advances in digital infrastructure and computing technologies allows for greater and greater value to be generated from the same amount of work. Think about how quickly you could write an essay by hand, versus typing it on your laptop, or even swiping it on your phone's keyboard. From this example, we can see that technological innovation has increased productivity and the associated potential value of working for an hour.

However, the gap between capitalist-class standards of living and working-class standards of living is clearly widening. The capitalists have projects in place to visit space as tourists, they have mansions and estates far larger and grander than anyone needs, they have mega-yachts that can house smaller yachts, and so on. Technology has enabled wonders in terms of living conditions, however, due to the extractive nature of capitalist wealth generation, the gap is ever larger. Capitalism didn't bring us any technology or its related improvements, the work of people did. Labor is what innovates.

Of course, there is a ton of negative propaganda and misinformation at all levels that obfuscates this. School curriculums and mass media are either directly or indirectly controlled by various members of the capitalist class, and their shared class interest is the maintenance of the system that gave them the codified right to their mind-bending wealth and its related privileges.

You might be wondering what all this has to do with fascism. We started this chapter discussing the economic nature of fascism. Economic relations cannot be separated from social ones. Fascism is the socioeconomic application of power to defend capitalism from some sort of crisis. Maybe that crisis is increased unionization, maybe it's a Marxist revolution, maybe it's simply dropping birth rates, or even a crisis of legitimacy where regular people begin to merely question the capital order. In the current moment, we are seeing three of those across Western society. In the US, for example, from the mid 2010s forward, union efforts have resurged. We've had wildcat strikes at colleges, we've had service workers like baristas and industrial workers like warehouse and fulfillment people go on strike, and even in some cases successfully join or start their own union. We've had increased discussion of "socialism", especially after Bernie Sanders' 2016 campaign for the presidency of the United States. (Despite Bernie calling himself and his policies socialist, on an accurate political charting he'd be considered a right-of-center reformist. His policies, if implemented, would serve to soften the harsh edges of capitalism and blow off economic pressures that might otherwise lead to more outright fascism or a socialist revolution.) And, as health and living standards increase, birth rates have been dropping.

The decline of birth rates is a sign of a post-industrial society. As living standards and political freedoms increase, the number of births needed to maintain or grow the population goes down and so too does the number of children people have. The number of people born but who died from stillbirth or didn't make it to adulthood pre-industrialization is far higher than any period after the beginning of the industrialization of a region. This is the living standards aspect. As far as political freedoms are concerned, the choice whether to get or remain pregnant, for example, directly impacts birth rates. The freer women and other people with uteruses are to choose, whether that choice is reproductive, economic, social, or something else, then the less successful the built-in coercive pressures of capitalist society are in forcing high birth rates.

All three of these, on their own, are crises for capitalism. The fact that all three are happening concurrently means that fascism must come out hard and swift in order to preserve the capital order. Just as there are workers sympathetic to capitalism, there are workers sympathetic to fascism. The exact number of working-class people who would engage in fascism to protect their creature comforts is incredibly high, and far higher than whatever number you're probably thinking of.

"Once more let me remind you what fascism is. It need not wear a brown shirt or a green shirt–it may even wear a dress shirt. Fascism begins the moment a ruling class, fearing the people may use their political democracy to gain economic democracy, begins to destroy political democracy in order to retain its power and special privilege." - T.C. Douglas

The ruling class mentioned above are the capitalists. In order to successfully pull off a fascist project (or even a capitalist one), the ruling capitalists require the support of the middle class (petit-bourgeoisie) and lower classes (working class). They acquire this support through coercion and through the offering of privileges. It's the age-old "carrot and stick" approach. The social fabric of western society has always enforced, violently, a rigid and essentialist view of sex and gender. Men have historically had access to disproportionate amounts of carrots while women have historically been forced to experience a disproportionate amount of sticks. This remains true today.

This social component of fascism is partially represented in the so-called "culture wars" of modern partisan political discourse. Unfortunately, both sides operate on reaction. The right-wing, reactionary red party and its base are reactionaries in the classical sense. The other right-wing, liberal blue party and its base often operate their opposition to the red party based on reaction. While liberals support the aesthetics and rhetoric of social reform, they are no less reactionary than the "other side" when it comes to economics.

The "conservative" side of the coin is pushing for repression and even extermination of queer people, starting with trans people and our ability to exist in public. The "liberal" side of the coin says they have our backs (President Joe Biden literally said "I got your back" to the trans community in an interview) but in reality they continually concede ground to the conservatives.

In the case of liberal concessions, they take many forms. It could be as simple as legitimizing the "trans debate" and its inherent dehumanization by engaging in actual debates with those architecting the anti-trans laws and programs. Sometimes it takes the form of repackaging transphobic arguments with social justice language. Worse still is when liberals who call themselves "allies" are asked to adjust their strategy or their language and immediately flip, or react, into supporting harm against trans people or even causing it.

As for the categorization of trans women as a threat, the reality is we are far more likely than cis women to experience misogynistic violence- including rape and sexual assault or harassment. In a study titled "Gender Identity Disparities in Criminal Victimization: National Crime Victimization Survey, 2017–2018" there were the following key findings:

- Transgender people (16+) are victimized over four times more often than cisgender people.
- Transgender women and men had higher rates of violent victimization than their cis counterparts within the gender binary.
- One in four transgender women who were victimized thought the incident was a hate crime compared to less than one in ten cisgender women.
- In 2017-2018, transgender households had higher rates of property victimization than cisgender households.
- About half of all violent victimizations were not reported to police. Transgender people were as likely as cisgender people to report violence to police.

As the key findings show, trans men and trans women are not only at greater risk of violence such as rape, assault, and domestic violence, but we are also at greater risk of structural violence such as evictions and other discrimination.

One of the study authors is cited saying the following:

"Research has shown that experiences of victimization are related to low well-being, including suicide thoughts and attempts. The results underscore the urgent need for effective policies and interventions that consider high rates of victimization experienced by transgender people." - Ilan H. Meyer

The violence we face as trans people is why we say in the community "every trans suicide is a murder". Nobody would commit suicide due to their transness if society wasn't so hostile to us in every way and across all realms of life. All the hardship that comes with transition is artificially enforced by a hostile system of cis-supremacy. Discovering or understanding yourself comes with joy, for anyone - cis or trans.

Trans joy persists in the face of a social and economic order and a cultural liberal hegemony that share the goal of reinforcing capitalism through repressing anything outside what is both acceptable and beneficial to the wealthiest capitalists. The idea that you can be something other than what you're told to be from birth is inherently dangerous to capitalism. This is the real threat trans people pose to the social order- the threat of free will.

# 6

The threat of free will.

DEATH, AND MEMORY.

*"Fascism is constructed"*

In order to understand why freedom of expression and choice is a threat to the status-quo, necessarily including patriarchy and capitalism, we must first understand the stratification of labor, gender segregation, and class antagonisms.

Trans people existing and going about our lives is a threat to the current social order because we reveal the hollowness of gender segregation and challenge the roots of euro-Christian patriarchal assumptions by merely existing and being visible as who we are. Why would a social order with its roots in European Christianity have such an aversion to free will, especially free gender expression?

The answer to that question dates back to at least the 12th Century with the Hereford Map. Extensive study on "non binary sex" has been done by others, including Leah Devun, such as in her book "The Shape of Sex: Nonbinary Gender from Genesis to the Renaissance". As discussed in that work, the Hereford Map was a way of defining the borders of the Christian world within Christian Europe, and things and places outside of the conceived borders of Christianity were weaved in as the "other".

Since at least the twelfth century CE, Eurochristian, gendered norms of social control have been strongly reinforced through the lens of "monstrous races" and the marginalization of non-binary sex and gender. (DeVun, 2021) Those norms relied on past establishments of patriarchal ideals that femininity meant softness, inferiority, uncleanness, and stupidity, where masculinity meant strength, domination, righteousness, and intelligence. Patriarchy wasn't an invention of Christianity, or twelfth century Europeans, but their version of patriarchy echoes today across the West.

If you can get a cis person to examine their beliefs about gender closely enough, and to be honest with you about those beliefs, you'll find that the core of cis understanding of gender is literally "belief". They don't tend to have grounded, material understandings of gender. They have a coercively constructed, white supremacist conception instead. This is true for most cis people, regardless of their individual race or other intersections with potential marginalization. In other words, nearly every person on this earth is primed by our societies to have a hollow, false, understanding of their internal experiences and other's experiences in regards to gender.

Not only are the vast majority of people walking around with internalized, crystallized beliefs regarding gender that are fundamentally wrong, Western society is, and has been, completely structured around violently enforcing compliance to those incorrect beliefs.

As for the stratification of labor, gendered labor divisions are inherently necessary to capitalism's functioning in the current moment, but also in the general history of capitalism as humanity's mode of production in any part of the world. Even as women of all kinds approach more equality and, sometimes, something close to equity in workplaces, the unwritten but loudly enforced assumption is that women will do the "feminine duties" and maintain the home, nurture the children, and overall carry the weight of their household and the overall economy on their backs. During the infancy of China's development towards socialism, Chairman Mao Zedong once said "Women hold up half the sky". I would offer a better, more accurate version today that echoes this sentiment- "Women hold up half the sky, but carry double its weight".

As for the construction of society: bathrooms, schools, sports, and recreational spaces are divided by the two cis genders. There is a clearly unexamined and obvious pattern of gender segregation across American society, the broader West, and even many non-Western societies. In America, the invisible work of women and AFAB people is the reason the economy can pretend to function. This assumption of free labor is inherent to capitalism but affects women incredibly disproportionately.

The patriarchy and its defenders, especially including so-called "gender criticals" "anti-trans activists" "trans criticals" and "TERFs" (or "trans exclusionary radical feminists"), as they brand themselves want you to believe that the two cis genders and the bimodal average of the two "usual" human sexes aren't only all that there is, but that men and males are essentially an entirely different species than women and females. In their imagining, gender and sex are rigid, unchanging, and derive your behavior and morals.

Of course, that is patently ridiculous. From a purely biological sciences standpoint, sex is variable. There are at least 6 known survivable pairings of human sex chromosomes, also known as karyotypes. 4 of those are considered intersex variations, but chromosome variations aren't the only way to be intersex or have a sex-variant body. Your primary sex hormone, whether testosterone or estrogen determines and modifies cellular and gene expression, even on hormone replacement therapy. All human life starts on a female template, which is why cis men have nipples. The male and female genitalia starts out as the same tissue in utero, and the presence of androgen (testosterone) during gestation is what triggers the growth of penis, scrotum, and testicles, pivoting from the development of uterus, ovary, and vulva using the same cells and original structures. The trigger for androgen surges that lead to the development of "male" genitalia in utero is the SrY gene, which is usally, but not always, located on the Y chromosome. Humans also have several different phenotypes. Primary and secondary sex characteristics in terms of appearance, size, and even function, are highly variable from human to human.

Reality is complex and messy, which is cool and fascinating but the truth of the messiness of our real world isn't always comforting, and it certainly doesn't fit into the Eurochristian hegemony and the ideology of Christianity in general. People turn to religion, in some cases, for the same reasons they turn to conspiracy theories. Both are more comforting than what is demonstrably real.

"Second, studies show that people rely more on conspiratorial thinking when they feel powerless. Counter-intuitively, clinging to a conspiratorial explanation of events gives people a sense of control. Since nefarious powers are at work behind the scenes, the thinking goes, I may not be able to actually influence events but at least I can see through the lies of the "official story." Subconsciously, we also find a sense of comfort in knowing that the world is not chaotic and that someone is in control, even if that someone is malevolent. Just as you'd prefer knowing where the spider is in the room to not knowing where the spider went, it can be comforting to know there's an order behind everything... even if it's a New World Order." - (Johnson, 2019)

From a social and physical sciences standpoint, hormones do not and cannot determine your behavior. They may effect physiological needs and urges but they do not control you. Patriarchy would force you to believe that testosterone is responsible for the violence of (cis) men and the domination of (cis) males in society, rather than let you critically examine patriarchy itself.

A cis, white, perisex, heterosexual, and able-bodied man is the standard by which all others are judged. This is to everyone's deficit, even, paradoxically, those privileged men. The lottery of birth, in other words the pure chance surrounding your birth, can determine your whiteness vs being a person of color, intersex vs perisex status, and, in many cases, your cisness and heterosexuality. Some queer people were born queer, others may have had their identities shift or change over time through socialization and/or trauma. All are valid. Queer people shouldn't (and therefore don't) need to defend how or why they're queer. Cisgender heterosexuals don't have to defend their sexual or gender identities and the associated expression.

And, yes, everyone has a gender and sexual identity.

Everyone, at least in terms of humans. I can't speak for the experience of other members of the kingdom of life. Of those buckets of identity status that intersect, which are- age, disability, race, gender, sex, perisex/intersex status, and sexuality, only one is unlikely to change over the course of one's life.

Being able-bodied is a temporary condition. On a long enough timeline, with enough life lived, every human has the inevitability of becoming disabled. Gender and sexuality are both fluid and can shift or change over different points in one's life. Biological sex, depending on how it's being measured, is also variable and somewhat fluid, especially with modern transition medicine. Being intersex, if not diagnosed at birth, might become diagnosed at the onset of natal puberty during one's teenage years or might go completely missed. (_Differences in sex development_ 2023) This one should be obvious, but you're never the same age for more than a moment. The constant passage of time is also constantly changing your age and its associated experiences, until you die. You were a different age when you started this paragraph than you are now at the end of this paragraph.

The only one of the, let's call them "identity buckets", that is unlikely to change over your life is race. Since race is a socially constructed category, the definition could theoretically shift enough within a single lifetime to exclude some persons from or include them into whiteness. Irish people weren't always considered white, for example. European and Jewish people also weren't always considered white, either. However, the lived experience, the trauma, the impacts, of that racialized experience won't disappear even in the unlikely scenario that the structures that caused them do.

Like any other social construct, being a social construct doesn't mean something is fake. Rather it means humans constructed it for or within the purposes of navigating and architecting our social realities and societies. There are tons of social constructs, and they are all nonetheless very real. Something that was created or built by humans doesn't cease to be real. In fact, we seem to give things we created more power over us than we do the natural world, at least in colonial/western societies.

Even within the broader queer community which, as a whole, faces disproportionate interpersonal and structural violence, trans people (especially trans femmes) face a disproportionately higher rate of violence against us as compared to the broader grouping of LGTBQ+ persons. This is even more true when you are trans and a person of color.

"Research shows that transgender people in the United States face persistent and pervasive discrimination and violence. According to the 2015 U.S. Transgender Survey—the largest national survey of transgender persons in the United States, with over 27,000 respondents—46% of respondents had been verbally harassed in the previous year, and 9% had been physically attacked as a result of being transgender (James et al., 2016). Nearly half (47%) had been sexually assaulted at least once during their lifetime. At work, 30% of respondents reported being fired, denied a promotion, or experiencing harassment including physical or sexual assault. And 40% of respondents had attempted suicide in their lifetime, which is nine times the rate within the general U.S. population. Transgender African Americans, according to research, are disproportionately impacted by violence among LGBT people. Among respondents to the 2015 U.S. Transgender Survey, 44% of Black respondents reported being verbally harassed, and more than half (53%) were sexually assaulted at least once in their life (James et al., 2016). Another study of anti-LGBTQ violence found that 71% of reported homicides were people of color, 52% were transgender or gender nonconforming, and 40% were transgender women of color (National Coalition of AntiViolence Programs, 2018).

LGBT people in the United States are particularly susceptible to violence and discrimination by law enforcement. LGBT people have historically been subject to heightened surveillance and victimization by law enforcement, and a study by the Williams Institute found substantial evidence that "LGBT individuals and communities continue to] face profiling, discrimination, and harassment at the hands of law enforcement officers" (Mallory et al., 2015).

For example, a 2014 report on a national survey of LGBT people and people living with HIV found that 73% of respondents had experienced in-person contact with police in the past five years, and of those, 21% experienced hostile attitudes from officers, 14% reported verbal assault by the police,

3% reported sexual harassment, and 2% reported physical assault (Lambda Legal, 2014). In the same survey, victims of crime reported inadequate police response to their reports of violence, with 205 respondents noting that they had filed formal complaints about police misconduct. Notably, police abuse and misconduct were reported at higher rates by respondents of color and transgender and gender non-conforming respondents." (Shaw, 2020)

"The suicide attempt rate among transgender persons ranges from 32% to 50% across the countries. Gender-based victimization, discrimination, bullying, violence, being rejected by the family, friends, and community; harassment by intimate partner, family members, police and public; discrimination and ill treatment at health-care system are the major risk factors that influence the suicidal behavior among transgender persons." (Virupaksha et al., 2016)

# 7

There are ten stages of genocide.

THERE ARE TEN STAGES OF GENOCIDE.

*"The Ten Stages"*

Scholars of genocide have analyzed the history of the Holocaust and determined that there are ten stages of genocide. These stages are-

1. Classification
2. Symbolization
3. Discrimination
4. Dehumanization
5. Organization
6. Polarization
7. Preparation
8. Persecution
9. Extermination
10. Denial

In the classification stage, differences between people and groups become less and less respected. A division is fostered between "us" and "them". The mechanism for this division can be through rhetoric and stereotypes that lead to social exclusion of those perceived to be different. During the symbolization stage, the hatred becomes visually manifested. For example, in Nazi Germany and the territories it occupied, Jews were forced to wear yellow stars to make it obvious that they were "different". To achieve the discrimination phase, the dominant group denies civil rights, citizenship, and/or social privileges to the identified groups. In 1935, the Nuremburg Laws stripped Jews of their German citizenship, which made it a crime for them to do many types of jobs and illegal to marry Germans who were non-Jews.

Dehumanization is carried out by treating the "other" outgroup with no assumption of dignity or rights. During the genocide against the Jews in WWII, the Nazis referred to Jews as "vermin". In the ongoing genocide against Palestinians by the Israeli government, officials have called Palestinians

THERE ARE TEN STAGES OF GENOCIDE.

"human animals" and "children of darkness". In the United States' campaign of genocide against the indigenous First Nations, indigenous people were referred to as "savages".

Organization is the planning and preparation for the destruction of a people or group. Genocides are always planned out in advance. Movements of hate become regimes of hatred through planning and organization, gaining power and normalcy as they go. As they do this, they train, war-game, and acquire weapons and other means of committing mass, mechanized violence. Persecution as a stage of genocide is when the victims of the incoming genocide are identified and put on lists. Then, people are often segregated formally or informally, such as through ghettos, camps, and prisons or through forced migration from one area to another.

Extermination is the culmination of all these prior stages. The hate group murders their selected target(s) through a deliberate, mechanized campaign of mass violence. Tens of thousands or even millions of lives are destroyed or ended. Genocide doesn't require mass death, it can achieved through erasing culture or changing beyond recognition the lives and lifestyles of the targeted group. (Holocaust Memorial Day Trust, 2020)
 [(The ten stages of genocide HMD Trust)](https://www.hmd.org.uk/learn-about-the-holocaust-and-genocides/what-is-genocide/the-ten-stages-of-genocide/)

Any one of these stages is often a declaration of intent to commit genocide and can be itself an act of genocide. In terms of the movement against trans lives, here are the stages of genocide in the linear order.

Classification (1st stage)-

Trans people, especially trans femmes and trans women were classified as "unsafe" to be around cis women. This manifested in language deliberately designed to seem like a "reasonable concern" while cloaking the true malice and intent behind the words. This is why transphobic rhetoric and anti-trans genocidal legislation has generally started with sports bans. It is also why particularly British-based TERFs (trans-exclusionary radicals who call themselves feminists) and gender critical (transphobes who pretend to be critical of a "gender ideology" and/or "the establishment" to garner sympathy) focus on the draconian and regressive UK definition of rape. This definition requires penetrative action with a penis in order for sexual aggravation to be considered rape. In the real world, cis women can rape cis men, and there are more ways than one to commit rape- regardless of what British law says.

Symbolization (2nd stage)-

In the UK, symbolization takes the form of a "GRC" or gender recognition certificate. It's a document required to be legally recognized as your gender if you are trans. Increasingly, you must carry it to conduct public activities or business without being discriminated against.

Hotels are now denying regular service to trans people in the UK, forcing them to use side entrances and forcing trans employees to have a GRC.

https://www.reddit.com/r/transgenderUK/comments/12srcoz/bad_news_from_the_hospitality_sector/

https://web.archive.org/web/20230423083822/https://www.reddit.com/r/transgenderUK/comments/12srcoz/bad_news_from_the_hospitality_sector/

Transphobes generally insist that they "can always tell" if a person is trans, however some have called for tattooing the foreheads of passing trans people.

Tulsi Gabbard's introduction of a federal bill to modify Title IX specifically so it would only protect the female category of funding for programs based on "biological sex" could very well be argued to be an opening salvo in the project of the domestic, internal genocide of trans people within the USA.%3E>

Polarization (6th stage)-

Propaganda disguised as "reasonable concerns", and "protecting women and children" circulates across mass media. More recent escalations in the form of state-level legislation in the United States cited articles published by the New York Times that aided the polarization stage of genocide. Christine Burns, author of Trans Britain, told Pink News the following:

"First it was folk like this saying 'we just have concerns'... 'we only want a debate'. Then there've been the parade of slogans: 'Adult human female'... 'Sex matters'... All the evidence points to them being a small minority but, over this time, their demands have become more chilling."

An article written by Emily Bazelon of the New York Times was cited by Missouri legislators in their successful attempts to pass anti-trans legislation. The anti-trans project in the current moment has had two primary methods of legislative discrimination. Those are bathroom bills and sports bans.

Bathroom bills require people to use gender-segregated bathrooms according to their assignment at birth, regardless of the presentation, gender, comfort, and safety of everyone involved. A trans man who fully passes- that is has reached a point of transition where he could be easily, readily, assumed to be cis, would be forced into the women's restroom- regardless of the comfort of the trans man or the majority cis women who use said restroom. Similarly, a trans woman who fully passes would be forced to use the men's restroom- regardless of her comfort or that of the majority cis men who use said restroom. Everyone in between or beyond the gender binary, regardless of "passing", presentation, comfort, and safety, would be forced to comply or face penalties as a sex offender. Being femme-presenting, especially as a trans woman, and going to the men's bathroom comes with a huge risk of harassment, assault, or murder at the hands of the cis men in said bathroom.

Passing is not the goal for every trans person, nor should it be. All people, whether trans or cis, should be safe to present how they are, and coercing trans people to pass as cis, to hide who they are, to maintain rights, liberties, and privileges is not simply violent cisnormativity, it is itself a form of the symbolization and discrimination stages of genocide.

Anti-trans sports bans are the other primary form of initial discrimination escalation. They are the Trojan horse by which extremists get the public on board with broader and more damaging forms of legalized and mandated discrimination. Those broader forms include denial of access to healthcare, denial of housing and employment protections, and disenfranchisement from public life through cross-dressing and/or drag bans. Drag bans in the current eliminationist project all share the quality of shoehorning anyone who is "cross-dressing", trans or cis, into the category of sex offender, even though wearing clothes is generally not a sexual offense. Cis women wearing pants under these laws would be sex offenders. They don't care about that, in fact- enforcing traditional dress norms that would forbid wearing pants as a woman is often seen as a "win", from their perspective.

Discrimination (3rd stage)-

Even in countries that are seen as more "progressive" regarding gender identity, many still have forms of legal discrimination.

Dehumanization (4th stage)-

Transmisogyny is older than modern languages. The very first transmisogynistic slur (that we know of) was "baeddel". That word is the reason we have the word "bad" in the modern era. Both the concept of "bad" and the word itself trace their roots to "baeddel". In the current fascist project, dehumanization takes many forms. From wojaks that caricaturize trans women to using the profile photos and other photos of trans people as "gotchas" or the basis of memes on social media, and to using slurs like "tranny" "troon" "shemale" and others, dehumanization of trans people, especially trans femmes is rampant. Trans men and trans mascs have it no less easy. They are made invisible or caricaturized as "lost lesbians", regardless of the actual trans person in question's sexuality.

Preparation (7th stage)-

In the current moment, the fascist project has prepared increased escalation in several ways. The literally hundreds of anti-queer state-level bills are just one of those ways. Another is normalizing civil violence against trans people. This is where the outrage against things like Dylan Mulvaney's Bud Light sponsorship comes into play for the fascists. Fascist elements made her more popular, for a time, on google trends than the president of the United States because she was in a social media post promoting the light beer.
![[Attachments/dylan mulvaney table.png]]

Organization (5th stage)-

Leaked emails prove that the architects of trans genocide orchestrated and organized through a small group of major players for years. It wouldn't be unfair to put this stage as the first chronological stage in the contemporary era. However, the stages continue and cycle. It's not merely a matter of what order they happen in with each genocide, it's about being aware of each stage so that society can safeguard against genocidal machinations regardless of how and when they manifest. Each stage can partially or fully coexist with any number of other stages.

A more current form of organization is the censure and removal of trans legislators this year. A high-profile case is that of Representative Zooey Zephyr of Montana. Via CNN:

"Montana's Republican-dominated House voted Wednesday to ban Rep. Zooey Zephyr, who had said GOP lawmakers would have "blood" on their hands for passing bills restricting transgender rights and rallied protesters Monday after Speaker Matt Regier blocked her from being recognized to speak, from the House chamber for the remainder of this year's legislative session.

Under the disciplinary measure approved on a 68-32 vote Wednesday, Zephyr – the 34-year-old Democrat from Missoula who last year became the first openly transgender woman elected to Montana's legislature – will be allowed to retain her seat and cast votes remotely. But she will not be able to participate in debates." - [(Bradner, 2023)](https://www.cnn.com/2023/04/26/politics/montana-house-bans-zooey-zephyr/index.html)

In that "rallied protestors Monday" line, CNN obscures that the protestors involved in standing for their rights to representation- and trans people's rights to exist were removed from the legislature floor by riot cops.
 [(Nicole Girten, 2023)](https://web.archive.org/web/20230427005542/https://dailymontanan.com/2023/04/24/let-her-speak-protesters-scream-arrests-follow-after-speaker-doesnt-recognize-zephyr/)>>

Denial (10th stage)-

At every stage, these elements have denied their intentions. Even now, they claim to criticize "gender ideology" rather than stating plain that they are talking about people. Human people. "The Trans Debate" is reheated branding of genocidal intent from "The Jewish Question" and "The Negro Problem"
 According to one of the more prominent architects of trans exclusion, described as a "gender critical activist" by most media sources, trans people are a "huge problem to a sane word".

"If you've got people – whether they're transitioned, whether they're happily transitioned, whether they're unhappily transitioned, whether they're detransitioned – if you've got people who've dissociated from their sex in some way, every one of those people is someone who needs special accommodation in a sane world where we re-acknowledge the truth of sex." - Helen Joyce (Kelleher, 2022

The "truth of sex" isn't what transphobic campaigners try to assert, as this book will illustrate. Even if human sex were binary, and it scientifically isn't, the types of behaviors and norms that gender criticals and the like try to enforce are all socially-driven, not purely biological instinct.

Symbolization (2nd stage)-

In the UK, symbolization takes the form of a "GRC" or gender recognition certificate. It's a document required to be legally recognized as your gender if you are trans. Increasingly, you must carry it to conduct public activities or business without being discriminated against.

Hotels are now denying regular service to trans people in the UK, forcing them to use side entrances and forcing trans employees to have a GRC.

https://www.reddit.com/r/transgenderUK/comments/12srcoz/bad_news_from_the_hospitality_sector/

https://web.archive.org/web/20230423083822/https://www.reddit.com/r/transgenderUK/comments/12srcoz/bad_news_from_the_hospitality_sector/

Transphobes generally insist that they "can always tell" if a person is trans, however some have called for tattooing the foreheads of passing trans people.

Tulsi Gabbard's introduction of a federal bill to modify Title IX specifically so it would only protect the female category of funding for programs based on "biological sex" could very well be argued to be an opening salvo in the project of the domestic, internal genocide of trans people within the USA.

DEATH, AND MEMORY.

![[Attachments/chapter header for _it all began with the sports_.jpg]]

Her bill, which was introduced on December 10th, 2020, created an environment for increased transphobia and so-called "reasonable debate" about the dignity, worth, and validity of trans lives, overnight. At the time, even though my egg hadn't cracked and I wasn't fully aware that I was a trans woman, I lost friends over defending trans people's rights. People who I considered political allies in the struggle for a better world went off on defending Gabbard's bill, even when I presented them with overwhelming evidence that the bill was unnecessary and discriminatory. Elite sports organizations already had provisions in place mandating certain extra steps for trans athletes that were scientifically-backed and accepted as "fair".

"Title IX was a historic provision championed by Hawai'i's own Congresswoman Patsy Mink in order to provide equal opportunity for women and girls in high school and college sports. It led to a generational shift that impacted countless women, creating life-changing opportunities for girls and women that never existed before. However, Title IX is being weakened by some states who are misinterpreting Title IX, creating uncertainty, undue hardship and lost opportunities for female athletes. Our legislation protects Title IX's original intent which was based on the general biological distinction between men and women athletes based on sex. It is critical that the legacy of Title IX continues to ensure women and girls in sports have the opportunity to compete and excel on a level playing field." - Former Representative Tulsi Gabbard, Press Release December 10th, 2022. %3Chttps://web.archive.org/web/20201211224546/https://gabbard.house.gov/news/press-releases/reps-gabbard-and-mullin-introduce-bill-ensure-title-ix-protections-women-and%3E

This was rightfully called out by trans people and few of our allies as a transphobic move. As we will discuss further in later chapters, there are several different types of "biologically male" and "biologically female" and transition medicine including HRT can and does move a trans person's body

## THERE ARE TEN STAGES OF GENOCIDE.

from one side of the binary to the other in many, even most, ways.

Anti-trans moral panic has used sport discourse and sport bans as its entry point. Fascists (describing themselves as feminists) who sought to increase societal expectations of women as inferior used "reasonable concerns" regarding "obvious biological differences" between stereotypically male and stereotypically female human bodies. These fascists called themselves, and still do, many things. They didn't just bastardize feminism, they also co-opted populism. Using a false populism to interject alt-right ideals into more mainstream acceptance has been a core component of the fascist strategy since Hitler and the Nazis decided to brand themselves as "national socialists". It may be inconceivable to many people today, but in the early 20th century, socialism was incredibly popular. Demands for production for the purpose of use and betterment of humans rather than privately hoarded profit were incredibly common and popular, at least relative to today's politics.

In light of this history, it is critical to note that the Holocaust was undeniably evil but not uniquely evil. The Holocaust was inspired by and built from the history of colonial displacement and genocide in service of "nation building" for settler-colonial projects such as the United States of America and Canada. History didn't stop after WWII, and that includes the legacy of genocide, as can be seen with Israel's occupation, erasure, and destruction of Palestine.

What made the Holocaust unique was that it was a genocide where the latest means of industrial production were applied to the systems of mass death- in other words it was an assembly line genocide.

# 8

It didn't start with stage one…

IT DIDN'T START WITH STAGE ONE...

*"The Stages Aren't Linear"*

It didn't start with classification, but classification did happen in order to further the aim of genocide against trans and queer people. It didn't start with classification because, in my view, the fascists and their allies genuinely thought their assumptions regarding the nature of trans people, especially trans women, were universally accepted as valid. It started with discrimination.

Transition medicine has always been gatekept. While countless professional organizations support transition-related care, including hormones and surgeries as a best practice for trans people with diagnosable gender dysphoria, the exact administration of transition-related medicine has been standardized by the WPATH, or the World Professional Association for Transgender Health Inc., which has formulated access to care as a series of hoops, jumps, and gates, so to speak.

While the newest edition of WPATH Standards of Care (SOC), which is WPATH SOC 8 did reduce the gatekeeping somewhat, the existence of WPATH as the dogmatic body determining the paths transition must take within medicine across the world is inherently a form of gatekeeping. This gatekeeping is not applied to cis people who seek medicine, even gender affirming care.

Yes, cisgender and cissexual people seek gender affirming care.

Cis men often seek gender-based treatments to address:
  - Male Pattern Baldness
  - Low Testosterone
  - Enlarged Breasts
  - Erectile Dysfunction
  - Body Aesthetics
  - Genital Function

- Fertility Issues

Cis women often seek gender-based treatments to address:
- Facial Hair
- Body Hair
- Breast Size
- High Testosterone
- Pregnancy
- Pregnancy Prevention
- Genital Aesthetics
- Body Aesthetics

Attempts to shame and stigmatize those cissexual individuals who seek treatments for these gender related issues exist. However, cisgender people who do undergo the relevant treatments don't face such outlandish legal punishments as jail time, being listed as a sex offender, and losing the right to vote (and other felon disenfranchisements). Trans people who seek gender affirming care have a relatively small segment of society advocating for all of these punishments, and more, and that group is succeeding in most U.S. states.

Beyond our medicine not being as freely and equitably accessible as compared to a cis person's medicine, even gender affirming care, the ongoing genocide of trans people in the "Western World" started with discrimination. As we've discussed, sports bans were used as the first step to lead to healthcare bans and full-on criminalization of transness. These bans of parts of our lives as well as our ability to exist in public should be considered a form of four separate stages of genocide simultaneously- discrimination, classification, dehumanization, and criminalization. All four of these stages of genocide exist simultaneously as the result of organization, which is the fifth stage of genocide in the list.

These laws, many of which have passed, in clear language, would and do

make it illegal and a criminal offense to:
  - give a trans person healthcare
  - exist in public while dressed in a way that is gender non-conforming (which affects cis and trans people)
  - treat a trans person with basic respect (use proper names and pronouns- something afforded to every cis person automatically)
  - be a good parent (if your kids is trans or expresses in any non-gender conforming way, you are committing child abuse under these types of laws)
  - interact normally with children (such as reading books to them or being in the presence of children while wearing clothes that don't comply with the encoded policing of gender)

Many of these laws make wearing clothes that don't comply with the fascist idealization of what a man or woman should wear a sexual offense, with the enhanced criminal penalties that entails- including registration as a sex offender.

- Are you a woman who wears pants? Congratulations, you are now considered to be a sex offender as dictated by on-the-books laws in multiple US states!

- Are you a man who wears loose shirts? Or even a kilt? Congratulations, welcome to prison and the sex offender's registry!

- Does your corporate employer require that you, a woman, wear ties? Are you a Geek Squad agent or a food-service employee? I'm sorry, but you're a sex offender now for showing up to work in uniform in the wrong United States state. Oh, and we'll send you to prison for a year, maybe more, because that's freedom, babe!

These scenarios are all based on real, on the books laws as well as laws that are being passed or have been written but not yet made law.

Of course, entrenched gender policing and hard, dogmatic rules on "what is a man" and "what is a woman" don't conflict with the right-wing perception of what the world should be. Even though these same ideals are unscientific and immaterial, the right-wing simply doesn't care. In fact, chewing up people and forcing them to reproduce and not express themselves in anyway other than the production of labor value to be siphoned into the hands of privateers is a feature for the right-wing imagination, not a bug.

Some of these laws even go further and legally define women as only those humans born assigned female at birth, currently possessing a uterus, and currently able to produce eggs. They are literally codifying into law that the only purpose and qualification of women is that of being a baby factory for men. The cruelty, and the control, are the point.

```
71      (f) "Female" means a person belonging, at birth, to the
72   biological sex which has the specific reproductive role of
73   producing eggs.
```

(Plakon, _House Bill 1521 - "CS/HB 1521: Facility Requirements Based on Sex"_ 2023)

This classification of what it is to be female came late in the game. Now that we're in the middle stages of genocide, the fascists feel comfortable wielding their power to commit this kind of classification into formal and enforced effect.

This has echoes in Nazi Germany.

If you didn't know, the Nazis passed hundreds of antisemitic laws within their first year of power. Most of them were arguably minor, even allowing for exemptions to the laws for popular groups. Many of those laws were even rolled back. Following this, the member of Hitler's cabinet who where more moderate, and weren't formally Nazis, convinced Hitler to reverse several policies through their reasonable arguments about benefits and impacts to Germany's economy.

These combined show us that movements of hate don't play the full deck right away. They instead prioritize the normalization of their hatred with smaller steps over time. They'll initially compromise because moving the needle at all means making the next hateful law even easier to justify. Additionally, those who ally with hateful movements in an attempt to moderate the worst evils, in other words to support the lesser evil, become complicit in the violence. The existence of "moderate" members of the hate movement make it easier to normalize and spread the mass violence.

Further, collaboration with a hate movement historically doesn't do anything but empower said movement. You can't give them an inch and use that to influence them away from their animus. "Doing the best we can in a bad situation" type of approaches actually enable things like genocide, as proven by the history of the Holocaust.

Groups like the Nazis, or the modern "Gender Criticals" would never gain enough power to carry out mechanized evils without the support of groups that ostensibly oppose genocide and similar projects.

We started with the discrimination in sports. These elements and their sympathizers knew that sports would be the perfect trojan.

Last I checked, adjectives are modifiers, not nullifiers. Generally they help describe something, and can help you understand the form of that specific example of that something, but they aren't generally used to say that something isn't actually what it is. In the English language, prefixes are generally used as nullifiers, not adjectives. An example:
    Word that indicates an object:

- Apple

The same word with adjectives in front of it:

- Red apple
- Mutant apple
- Green apple
- Tri-color apple
- Sliced apple
- Eaten apple

The same word with a prefix indicating that the object being indicated is not a certain object:

- Non-apple

See what I mean?

Of course, language itself is fluid and descriptive, rather than prescriptive, so this conception could change but, holding to the rule we just explored, the adjectives "trans" or "cis" and, in their prefix form with the words "transgender" and "cisgender", are giving us a more detailed description of someone. A cis woman is a woman. A trans woman is a woman. The adjectives don't change the fact that both are women, rather give us more detail of what kind of woman we're describing. Is a happy woman not a woman?

As for other words that use the latin words "trans" and "cis", beyond transgender and cisgender, which each date back decades, we have, in no complete or particular order:

- translator
- cislunar
- cistern
- cisatlantic
- transact
- transport
- transcribe
- transcend

and so on... and so on... If you're interested in all the words that start with trans and/or cis, I suggest procuring a copy of the English-Language dictionary.

The next paragraph pathologizes being trans as a mental disorder and engages in ableism. It says that "we" and "the state" shouldn't affirm a "delusion". Here's the thing: being trans does not equal being delusional.

In fact, trans people have always existed across societies and throughout human existence. The word itself that we use today to describe the collection of experiences in being transgender hasn't always existed, but neither has the English language or the Christian Bible they're using to try and justify our extinction. In fact, as we'll discuss in a later chapter, the conceptions of sex and gender that these anti-trans elements fall back on are a blend of 12th-14th century Eurochristian conceptions. Those conceptions served the purposes of defining the Christian world, in terms of territory and social norms, and also served to reinforce the power of a rising theocratic, or clerical, aristocracy.

If you are skeptical that Christianity is a motivator for this project of genocide, please re-consider. My heritage is Mormonism, which is a restorationist sect of Christianity, my family and ancestors have been Mormons since Mormons existed. Before that, my ancestors were still Christians, and before that they were Celtic pagans. As a part of the greater realm of Christianity, I had to learn to deconstruct my original faith and the culture I came from, was raised in, and was originally molded by.

Let us also address detransitioning, or what the anti-trans elements and their supporters call "desisting". Those who detransition, and let's call them "detrans persons", should be entitled to same amount of medical care as a cis person or trans person. Everyone should have universal access to equitable healthcare that isn't pay to play, in other words- that is free at the point of service.

Universal, high-quality, free healthcare is entirely possible. It doesn't require raising taxes, and in the United States of America- it would be deflationary. (Barber, 2019)

In addition, transition medicine regret rates are a combined total of 1-2% of everyone who transitions. (Castagnaro, 2023) (Wamsley, 2022) (Bustos et al., 2021) (Chen et al., 2023) In addition, almost the entirety of those who detransition, do so so because of external pressures, such as the social, legal, and financial costs and penalties enforced on trans people who pursue transition.

Think about this: If there were a treatment for cancer that cured, or at least successfully treated cancer (or diabetes, or most other medical conditions) and led to better quality of life for the patient 98-99% of the time, it would be rightfully considered a miracle cure and research and publicity would be poured into expanding the rate the breakthrough treatment was used. In real life, today, transition medicine has a non-theoretical, actual 98-99% success rate in saving lives and enhancing quality of life, and Christians, fascists, and even some self-styled "feminists" are pouring their every effort into criminalizing it, banning it, and destroying any knowledge of it.

Detransition rates are roughly 12.9% of those who transition. However, more than 8 out of 10 detrans people (82.5%) only detransitioned due the coercion of external factors. 10.8% of those who transition in the current environment will detransition permanently due to the hostility of cis supremacy and the social, legal, financial and other burdens and costs artificially imposed on us. For some, the forceful and harsh costs cis people put us through when we decide to pursue our own joy and happiness are too much to bear. Only 2.1% of people who pursue medical transition permanently detransition due to their own internal choices alone. (Turban et al., 2021)

Transition medicine has a 98-99% success rate and only less than 11% of people who pursue transition-related treatment stop pursuing that treatment, and of those who stop, only 2.1% of all transition medicine patients stopped permanently due to an internal choice. This means that 9 out of 11 or more people who detransition or stop pursuing further transition do so because they were coerced and/or forced into stopping or detransitioning.

Let us be clear: The true motivation of transphobic concerns about detransition rates is only motivated by a feeling of supremacy. Cis people, or at least those who are transphobic, would generally rather that 1 cis person is prevented from pursuing a gender transition and regretting it even when it means a million dead trans people. To most cis people, we aren't human- we aren't even close to human. The conception of non-binary and trans sex or gender being "monstrous" dates back to at least The Hereford Map (DeVun, 2021) For us, it's a common experience to be treated well and just like anyone else by a cis person, up to and until the point where the cis person in question finds out you are trans.

Hurt cis feelings, and the avoidance of having them, are infinitely many times more valuable than the preservation of trans lives in the collective cis imagination. I understand if you, as a cis person reading this aren't trying to be a part of that, or even believe you aren't a part of it. It's a similar phenomenon to women saying "men suck" due to the history and current reality of violence, abuse, and death men direct towards us women. Sure, it's not all men, but it's enough of them, and could be any of them at any time. The same holds true for how cis people treat trans people.

# 9

# A brief history of "experimental" medicine.

DEATH, AND MEMORY.

*"Understanding the Backslide"*

Trans people are fighting regression. Nearly every right and privilege that has been a topic of discourse is neither new, nor experimental. HRT, puberty blockers, surgeries, social transition, name changes, even limited gender marker changes have all existed with relative levels of legal and clear access for years to decades or longer.

However, in recent years, anti-trans elements have used debate and media appearances to whip up a transphobic moral panic. The fact that trans people have always existed, and the fact that every medical technology trans people use for medical transition was pioneered first for cis people is not considered. Instead, they echo a drumbeat of "danger to children" and use every tactic they can to associate queerness, especially transness as an inherent threat to civil society.

Calling it the "trans debate" and criticizing what they call "trans ideology" is a cover for what they are really attempting. This so-called "trans debate" is just a 21st century version of the "negro problem" or the "Jewish question". People aren't debatable. Debates are for sharpening rhetoric and deepening positions, and should not be used as a means by which anyone dehumanizes any marginalized group.

So called "anti-trans activists", "gender criticals" and "TERFs" (the names of groupings of the anti-trans elements mentioned above) use debate and co-opted social justice language via a sympathetic media apparatus to come across as only possessing "reasonable concerns". This is how they are obfuscating their true intentions. To engage in debate regarding people, human beings living their lives without harming anyone is to engage in, at minimum, one of the ten stages of genocide - dehumanization. (More on the ten stages of genocide later.)

As for trans surgery, vaginoplasty was pioneered first for cis women who had malformed vaginas or were in some sort of accident that damaged their genitals. The same holds true for phalloplasty. The construction or re-construction of a penis was designed first for cis men who experienced an injury in their genitals.

The first male-to-female vaginoplasty was performed in 1931. This surgery was performed at Hirchfield's Insitut for Sexualwissencraft (which we will discuss in more detail later). That surgery was the world's first recorded sex-change surgery. The first trans person known n to receive mass-media attention was Christine Jorgensen, who underwent a sex-change operation or, as we'd call it today, "gender affirming bottom surgery" in 1952.

By contrast, the world's first open heart surgery wouldn't be performed for another 3 years from the time Christine Jorgensen made mass-media news because she received gender-affirming surgical care. A Dr. Kilkin performed this heart operation. The groundbreaking cardiac surgery took place at Rochester Methodist Hospital, and the operation was made possible through a machine called the "Mayo-Gibbon heart-lung machine". This heart-lung machine assumed cardiorespiratory functions for a 5-year old girl named Linda Stout, who was from North Dakota. This mechanical takeover of biological functions allowed the surgical team lead by Dr. Kilkin to correct a heart defect and save the girl's life.

**Sex-change genital surgery is literally older than open heart surgery by 44 years.**

Puberty blockers have been prescribed to people of relevant ages, as medically necessary, for decades. Puberty blockers have been known to be safe since at least the 1980s. There are some extreme cases of depleted bone density, but those don't really happen anymore, provided proper administration is undertaken. The risks of severe side effects only present if someone is on puberty blockers too far in time past their natal puberty.

The issue that trans healthcare presents isn't one of "risk" or "danger" in the way anti-trans reactionaries would you have believe. They want you to believe that medically appropriate care that has been in use for decades is suddenly a "danger to children" despite it being used on children in those same timelines because freedom of expression and bodily autonomy -together the freedom of the self- are an inherent threat to their fascist goals. They obfuscate this, of course, because they know if they were fully honest with their goals from the beginning, they wouldn't get far.

This fundamental attack on freedom of the self underpins the overall fascist movement. Freedom of expression, bodily autonomy, freedom of association, and what I call choice sovereignty are all seen by fascists as aberrations at best, criminal evils at worst. Choice sovereignty is the concept that every human has a right to their inner selves and their outer selves, as well as every possible and reasonable choice regarding their reality. If a human being wants to change their body, or change their job, or change their family, or change where they live, they should be allowed to without question. Society should accommodate these freedoms. Rather than merely tolerating human choice, the idealized society would encourage and foster it.

If we aren't free to choose who we are, if there are forces of social, legal, or financial consequence that interfere with free expression of the self, that is a very real and palpable type of prison. For queer people, the closet doesn't grant privileges, it is an enclosure. Unlike the kinds of prisons normalized in Western society, the closet is usually guarded and enforced by the very people closest to you, who not only claim to care the most for you in their words but also hold the most direct power over the trajectory of your life through their deeds.

Trans people are under constant coercion in the current socioeconomic system. Transitioning nearly always comes at a great cost, with the burden being spread across the realms of social, legal, familial, material, and financial consequence. Trans women earn the least out of any group, averaging 60 cents to a cis, white, heterosexual man's dollar for the same work. Non-queer cis women, on the other hand generally earn on average of 83.7 cents to the cis, white, non-queer man's dollar. *Trans women are paid the least compared to the typical worker out of any minority group.* Some other examples of this pay gap include trans men and LGTBQ+ or queer indigenous workers, who make 70 cents on the "typical" worker's dollar. Non-binary and two-spirit individuals generally make 80 cents on the "typical" worker's dollar, as do the people who are both queer and black.

Like all freedoms, there are limits on choice sovereignty. If you use your freedom of choice to directly harm someone else, and that someone else isn't harming another or yourself, there should be some sort of consequence. Maybe rehabilitation, maybe re-education, maybe just needing to apologize and make an effort at restoration. The thing is, the only people who see queerness and transness as inherently violent or as an assault on their being are people who are either fascists themselves or misguided fundamentalists that believe that their rights include a false right to never be exposed to difference.

Often, this false "right" is presented through co-opted and bastardized social justice language. For example, cis women who are among the TERFs and so-called gender-criticals often say they "don't consent to men in our spaces". In doing so, they are actually saying they don't consent to being reminded of the existence of trans women. We know that this is their true meaning because they often include transmisogynistic slurs, such as "TiM" or "TIM"- their term for "trans-identifying male". This slur simultaneously denies a trans woman's existence, validity, and humanity. We are not males, and saying we "identify as women", for example, is actually a microaggression. We are women. We live as women. Everything a trans woman does is something a woman does, because we are, and always have been, women. Both "cis" and "trans" are adjectives. They clarify and add description to the terms they are used with, but do not negate them.

Consent doesn't apply when we're talking about the existence of other humans. You don't get to revoke consent to the fact that I exist. All else being equal, you can choose not to affiliate with me, but wrapping the language and concept of consent around whether or not I, or anyone else, should exist is inherently violent.

## A BRIEF HISTORY OF "EXPERIMENTAL" MEDICINE.

"We can disagree and still love each other unless your disagreement is rooted in my oppression and denial of my humanity and right to exist."
— James Baldwin

# 10

# The Chair Paradox

"The Chair Paradox" is a term for a phenomenon observed by trans people forced to debate their validity in social media spaces. It's actually pretty simple. There is no single definition of a "chair" that includes everything that is a chair and excludes everything that isn't a chair. The same is true of womanhood. There is no single definition of women that includes every cis woman while excluding every trans woman. Of course, trans women are women. We are women across the spectrum, biologically, socially, and so on.

The veracity of the chair paradox can be proven pretty simply. The standard definition of a chair is something along the lines of "something suitable for human seating, with four legs and a back".

May I present, a chair!

THE CHAIR PARADOX

[ Fine portrait of a horse by F Humphrey, Brockford, Suffolk" by whatsthatpicture is marked with Public Domain Mark 1.0. ]

Obviously, horses aren't the same thing as a chair. You can't simply define a chair in a way that includes all chairs while excluding all non-chairs, as we can see. Our single simple definition of a chair clearly includes horses.

May I present, not a chair!

DEATH, AND MEMORY.

[ "'Almost Hobbes' the st tiger, Really Likes this Beanbag Chair at Target! Taken by Mike Mozart!" by JeepersMedia is licensed under CC BY 2.0. ]

Another object that clearly isn't a chair!

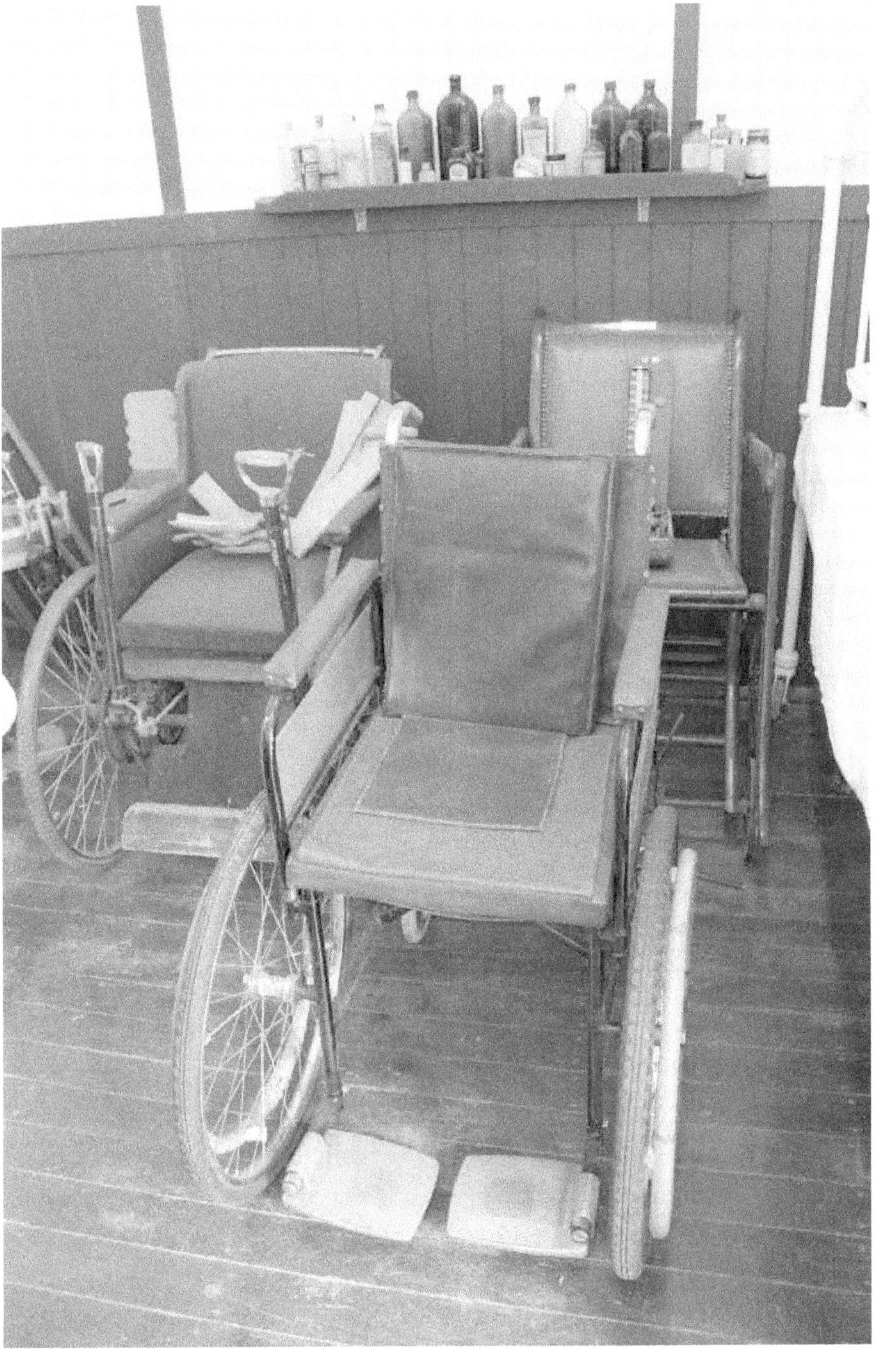

[ "Collection of wheel chairs at Crystal Brook Heritage Centre" by South Australian History Network is marked with CC0 1.0. ]

As we have seen, the inverse is true. Even if we only look at actual chairs, our simple definition of a chair would exclude them. The same is true for both men and women. No one definition of manhood or womanhood could ever possibly include all men (or women, respectively) and exclude all things and people that aren't men (or women, respectively).

Sex and gender are both on separate, but linked, bimodal distributions. Here is an example of a bimodal distribution:

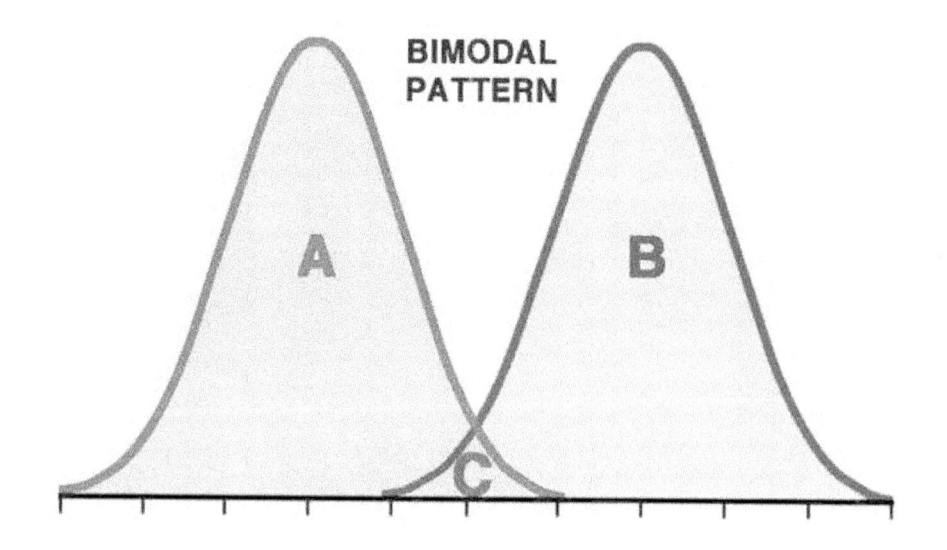

**BIMODAL PATTERN**

A  B  
C

As you can see, there are two primary categories, A, and B. The more common traits within either category are more prevalent. The more individuals that share these traits, the more they would show up on the chart. Category C represents examples of overlap between traits commonly found in one of the other of the two bimodal poles. In the case of human sexes, "Category C" would refer to anyone who is intersex.

The bimodal distributions of "male" and "female" while linked socially to those of "man" and "woman" are not identical. There's overlap, and connectivity, but as terms like "male" or "female" are biological constructs while "man" or "woman" are social constructs, they cannot be defined or charted in exactly the same manner. In terms of biology, there are 6 currently known survivable pairings of sex chromosomes, not just the two you might have learned about in school. They are:

- X – Roughly 1 in 2,000 to 1 in 5,000 people (Turner's Syndrome)
- XX – Most commonly considered to be "female"
- XXY – Roughly 1 in 500 to 1 in 1,000 people (Klinefelter Syndrome)
- XY – Most commonly considered to be "male"
- XYY – Roughly 1 out of 1,000 people
- XXXY – Roughly 1 in 18,000 to 1 in 50,000 humans born

This of course, is before you consider cellular expression and the possibility of mosaicism. It is entirely possible for the cellular structures that comprise your brain, your body, and your reproductive system to each have different karyotypes- that is, different sexes.

Regardless of how you were born, how you now present, and regardless of your identity, cis or trans, you personally have no way of discovering on your own what your karyotypical sex is. Many transphobic arguments boil down to the bio-essentialism of "man = XY and woman = XX, duh!". However, reality is far messier, cooler, and more expansive. The nature of our world and universe, and the scientific understandings that help us comprehend them never fit into a simple box, or a simple binary system. There is variability in everything.

None of us know our "biological sex" in the context transphobic elements use the term, except for the very few of us who have undergone chromosomal typing and genetic testing specifically to find out what our karyotype, or chromosome pairing is. When transphobes talk about "biological sex", they are often speaking about chromosomes.

However, chromosomes don't determine your identity. They don't dictate your behavior. They don't instill you with your core beliefs. Your karyotype can help explain some aspects of your physical body and how it developed, but it does not determine who you are.

## 11

## Whiteness is hegemonic.

This story is from one of the jobs I've had over my life so far. I was working for a large, international, shipping and freight company as an entry-level warehouse worker. More specifically, I was one of many humans helping move cargo and packages from belt to belt or belt to truck and so on.

During a normal shift in the middle of the night (3am was a typical start-shift time), as we were getting set up for our work, one of my colleagues who was a woman got very upset with another woman who was working in the same area as us two. This white lady was verbally harassing towards the other lady, who was black and wore clothes covering most of her body and head, I assume for religious or cultural reasons.

Now before you make any assumptions, here is what led up to this moment: The white lady, let's call her Karen (not her real name) arrived first. She was setting up our shared workspace for shared use. The black lady, let's call her Yvonne (also not her real name) arrived and began to prepare the final steps for our shared workstation. Seeing that Karen got the sort buckets and sort belt in the right positions, it seemed logical that Yvonne would work on getting the scanning and printing equipment going.

However, this was not seen as acceptable by Karen. Karen seemed to feel that, basically, Yvonne was stealing her work. This frustration was because Yvonne was setting up in a fashion that Karen didn't like. It wasn't the wrong way, it was how I'd always seen Yvonne do it on our other shifts. All that was "wrong" with the way she was doing it was that it was slightly different than how Karen wanted it done.

Now, none of us in this scenario were managers, supervisors, or even trainers. We were all functionally equal in the corporate hierarchy. Yet, Karen lost it when someone did something outside of the way she saw fit. The harassment and rage that followed is a part of our story as much as the fact that it made getting work done that shift all the harder for all of us.

Some of what made the shift harder was that Karen couldn't let it go. She spent more time yelling at Yvonne or trying to flag down a manager than she did actually scanning and sorting packages at her station. She also spent a significant portion of the shift trying to get me to agree with her. Some of that was non-verbal eye communication, like eye-rolls and other gestures to try and get me to share in the expression of frustration. The rest was telling Yvonne or myself what to do and using a forceful voice to try and make us perform her way of doing tings.

This example is a tiny microcosm of the concept we are discussing in this chapter. Whiteness is a system of social control via social, political, and economic exclusion. It is also hegemonic.

Whiteness is a system. As a system, as all of those forms of influence it is also the maintenance of such influence. In our example, all 4 forms of influence were at play. Karen attempted to wield each of them throughout this shift.

- Social: Trying to get me, a fellow white coworker to agree with her and support her "my way or the highway" approach is a form of attempted social influence.
- Cultural: Trying to get a manager to enforce her way of doing things is

## WHITENESS IS HEGEMONIC.

both cultural and economic. As for cultural influence, trying to coerce Yvonne and the rest of the team to do it her way through the force of a manager's word is a form of trying to affect workplace culture.
- Ideological: The core of Karen's issue in this situation was ideological. Without extrapolating to possible racism, the central issue Karen had was that things weren't being done the way she wanted and saw as the right way, across the workspace.
- Economic: By involving a manager and trying to get Yvonne in trouble, Karen was wielding economic influence because if Yvonne had lost her job, or had hours reduced, or some other negative reinforcement due to Karen's pleas with the manager, those would've all effect Yvonne's economic situation.

Now, I want you to imagine that a version of this micro-example happens thousands, if not millions of times a day across all sorts of interactions, because it does. Ask yourself:

1. Why does this interpersonal policing of labor being done happen so much if the work gets done either way?
2. Why do some people feel empowered to be harassing and abusive towards another human over slight disagreements?
3. Why does the abuser think that the powers involved in the situation will side with them?

One of the answers to all three questions, and the one we are focusing on for the rest of this chapter is- "Whiteness is hegemonic."

Being "white" is socially constructed by the ruling class. It always has been. Irish people weren't always considered "white", because it was more acceptable to have an additional division of the specifically white subgroup of the overall working class in order to artificially suppress the pay and wages workers received. Capitalism isn't merely about greed and profit, there is also a great deal of contempt for the worker by those same capitalists at the top of the system. Capitalists hate workers.

The concept of race, as we know it today, was an invention to justify the continuance of slavery and the establishment of the chattel form of slavery by European powers and then the new United States. This creation of the notion of separate races based on skin tone has had far-reaching effects in every aspect and era of United States history. Racism drives transphobia, but it also drives economic misery, and many other evils.

Public school, especially public tertiary education became systematically defunded and deprioritized in response to the end of segregation. The for-profit model of medicine we have today in the United States was also created in response to the end of segregation and in order to maintain racist outcomes.

In addition to the interpersonal conflicts empowered by the system of whiteness, also known as white supremacy, living under a white supremacist system doesn't mean "lots of white supremacists in the system". Rather, it means "even if there were zero white supremacists in the system, it will still produce racist outcomes against those not socially considered to be white while unfairly elevating those who are socially considered to be white".

An example of whiteness as a system is the fact that there are more African Americans in slavery, today, right now, in the United States, than at the height of chattel slavery. The US prison system is crystallized and reified modern slavery. Mass incarceration as we have it today was architected by then Senator, now President Joe Biden. (Biden also drafted the legislation that eventually became the PATRIOT Act, creating the modern mass surveillance state.) Biden has always walked a fine tightrope between neoliberal (soft fascism) and outright fascist. In addition, 25% or more the world's prison population is in the United States, whereas the US only has less than 5% of the global population. We are number one in militarism, imprisonment, and propaganda. The US leads the world with nothing of merit. The subject of prison labor as a modern form of slavery could fill a small library, and I couldn't possibly do the subject in its entirety justice in this book. Yet, while we're on the topic, Vice-President Kamala Harris, in her former role as DA, deliberately and illegally extended prison sentences and delayed release of prisoners so that they could be used as slave labor for the state of California to fight wildfires. Yes, a capitalist, even a self-styled "progressive" liberal (still capitalist) government enslaved people, this is essential to the functioning of capitalism.

As for the intersection of transphobia and racism, African cultures pre-colonialism often had several gender roles. There were also several different ways of gender expression and matriarchal society was a common setup. A similar reality existed in many indigenous cultures here in North America.

By the era of colonialism, any framework for liberatory thought sourced from any mass understanding of Christianity had been subsumed by centuries of the merger of state and church power. Any gender-expansive reading of "There is no male or female, for ye all are one in Christ Jesus" as it is written in the book of Galatians, along with most of the core teachings one can derive from the story of Jesus Christ's life, had been swapped with domination, might, and empire. Christianity was progressive, back when humanity was transitioning to feudalism from the forms of slavery and caste that came before. It isn't anymore.

# 12

# Transmisogyny is the economy.

Dehumanization takes many forms. For trans women, that form is chiefly one of monsterization and hypervisibility. Trans men, on the other hand are made invisible or sometimes caricaturized as "lost lesbians", regardless of the actual trans person in question's sexuality. Transmisogyny is the mechanism by which trans women are dehumanized. Broadly speaking, the transphobic hate movement does dehumanize all trans people. It does this by conflating our existence with that of a cult, or mental illness. However, the common thread of transmisogyny creates an environment where non transfemme trans people are constructed as victims of the cult or illness, and transfemme trans people are painted as the manipulators or infectors.

"If you've got people – whether they're transitioned, whether they're happily transitioned, whether they're unhappily transitioned, whether they're detransitioned – if you've got people who've dissociated from their sex in some way, every one of those people is someone who needs special accommodation in a sane world where we re-acknowledge the truth of sex." - Helen Joyce (Mirkinson, 2022) (Kelleher, 2022)

Helen Joyce historically focuses her rhetoric and her constructions of what "should be" against trans women. However, she does so by attempting to strike a middle-ground of her own making. In contrast to some of those in the same patriarchal currents as her, she is given credit by her peers for admitting that trans people go through pain and suffering, but she only does so to the degree that it helps her pathologize our existence. In a review of one of her works written by the anti-trans journalist Jesse Singal, this so-called middle ground between:

1. trans people managing to unfortunately exist despite the artificial limitations on being able to, which in their words is, "trans rights"

and-

2. trans people standing up for themselves and advocating for freedom and human rights, which is, in their words "gender-identity ideology"

makes Helen Joyce, in Signal's words, a "intelligent, thorough" thought-leader for the trans-exclusionary patriarchal movement that calls itself either "trans exclusionary radical feminist" or "gender critical". (Singal, 2021)

In Janice Raymond's *The Transsexual Empire (1994 edition)*, she states that "transsexualism remains as in 1979, largely a male phenomenon. Female-to-constructed male transsexuals are relatively rare." In the same passage, Raymond waxes long about how hormone replacement therapy, is inherently dangerous due to her assertion of a high risk of cancer and "health and safety complications". In this part of the passage she focuses specifically on "lifelong exogenous estrogens taken by male-to-constructed female transsexuals". (Raymond, 1994) Hormone therapy does in fact not create higher risks of cancer in trans women than their cis women counterparts. Breast cancer rates, for example, are far lower for trans women on HRT for their lives as compared cis women (who have similar estrogen levels without going on HRT). (de Blok et al., 2019) (Gardner & Safer, 2013) Raymond's statements require an unexamined approach to trans women's hyper-visibility and trans men's hyper-invisibility, which Raymond herself takes part in constructing.

However, there is a difference contrasting invisibility with forced victim-hood versus hyper-visibility with forced monsterization. Non transfemme trans people, owing to their invisibility and automatic victim-hood granted by both liberal validity politics and trans exclusionary radical feminists, dominate the power structures within trans and queer spaces. Non transfemme trans people are dehumanized through infantilization as victims to be protected, and most inclusion efforts focus on them while reactionaries generally direct the backlash for having those inclusion efforts at transfemme trans people.

Trans women are, like all women, subjected to extreme patriarchal violence. However, unlike many cis women, we cannot fulfill the primary role relegated to the woman gender owing to cis men's inability to replace women for the purposes of childbirth and gestation. The woman gender is constructed so as to be not what men are. Of course, our ideas of the man gender are equally constructed. This doesn't mean that they aren't real, but rather they were built. Traditional gender roles and the patriarchy that enforces them were built by humans, and are maintained by humans. There is no divine decree nor natural law that manifests as brute facts that requires the existence of patriarchy in all its manifestations.

In the Western world, patriarchal violence against trans women includes men that will desire us sexually but murder us the second he's "found out" for being into us. It includes being policed and having every word we say being taken in absolute bad faith. It includes v-coding, which is the practice of putting trans women in men's jails and making her share a cellmate with known violent prisoners in order for our bodies to be used as an object that mellows out the violent cis male prisoner through state-sanctioned rape. It includes all other sorts of misogynistic treatment, intensified by the fact that trans women are women who cannot serve a woman's only valid purpose within patriarchy- we cannot, without intervention be a baby making machine. Trans women are women that are dehumanized to the point where they can be understood as women that face the worst patriarchal violence- without women's networks, women's supports, or the consensus that we are in fact victims. In other words, we face incredible patriarchal violence without the recognition of our womanhood. Being recognized as like gender and a fellow human by other women is what gives victims of patriarchal violence access to supports. Those supports are constructed despite patriarchy, in the face of it, and come from women of all kinds pooling their resources, access to social and cultural capital, and their experiences and intragender knowledge.

In the global south and the so-called "Third world", largely due to the legacy of colonialism and the ongoing state of imperialism and extraction-ism, trans women and their third-gender analogs face an intensification of the conditions Western trans women face, as well as some unique manifestations of violence owing to their own regional and cultural histories of patriarchy. Patriarchy often pre-existed before capitalism, and before the colonialism that followed in its wake to sustain the capitalist mode of production.

Women's networks and spaces are understood to be ground gained by feminists across history. However, the exclusion of trans women from those networks and spaces are a conclusion of anti-feminist action within and without feminist movements. Cis-sexism and sex essential-ism are choices in ideology that were made by certain key feminists of the past, undermining their own liberation to stick it to trans women. The wins of feminist spaces include women's suffrage and legal recognition as independent human beings (for the most part) in countries like the USA, yet trans women were and are excluded from those same "wins". It is also important to note that every win gained by feminism this far is largely conditional and can be rolled back by the ruling class and its instruments of capitalist state power at any time.

As of 2023 and into the beginning of 2024, in the United States, there is still no federal recognition of trans women as women, and no federal protections against discrimination exist to broadly protect trans people. In fact, most "red states" are advancing their laws and statutes ensuring discrimination and preventing legal recognition. (Migdon & Manchester, 2023) (Rummler, 2024) It's still legal in a super-majority of states (33!) to kill a trans person and claim the infamous "panic" defense, which may allow you to get away with literal murder because you claimed that knowing your victim was trans made you frightened. (Ring, 2023) The panic defense is a much older consequence of dehumanization.

Outside of the US, trans women face similar types of violence that is often more intense and reified, with less recourse. Some USian trans women can flee to one of the safer states. I did. However, in non-US patriarchies that isn't usually the case. In the global south, trans women can expect to be subjected to the most extreme practices of sexual exploitation and human trafficking in far greater rates than in the global north. Validity for trans women in certain regions is being allowed to live as long as they are the product for foreign men to come and abuse and rape via sex tourism.

Taken together, the reality is that trans women are forced to become sexual objects for violent men. When TERFs and gender criticals call our existence a fetish, they are only acting to reinforce the forcing of us from normal public life into the fringes where the patriarchal demands regarding women's sexual availability become the only experience we receive. Seeing as trans women cannot without intervention and advanced medicine get pregnant, we're the "perfect" receptacle for sexual violence and trafficking. Pimps and their ilk don't have to worry about access to abortions or clothes hangers, because we are by definition infertile women. Sex traffickers also don't have to worry about what will happen in terms of institutional consequences to the same degree. This is because trans women are the most acceptable targets of patriarchal violence. We face the brunt of it at all times, across places, nations, and times.

Transmisogyny can be further understood, in part, as a scalpel to cut up the body called women, comprised of the woman genders and create a rift in the organ of feminism between trans women and cis women. This rift is like a surgical wound without a suture, it only grows and festers if not forcibly stitched together in an ongoing process while new tissues are synthesized by the body. Without cleaning and a new suture for healing, this surgically inflicted wound will eventually kill the body that was forced to experience it.

Similarly, generalized transphobia and the attacks on trans mascs can be understood through the spaces that they are offered within both patriarchy and queer institutions. Trans men and transmasculine people are offered a space, however tenuous, within patriarchal movements. TERFs are especially effective at recruiting non trans woman / femme trans people into patriarchal fealty if they detransition and use their own bodies as ammunition against trans people by aiming the weapons of rhetoric and their experiences against trans women. It is an entire pipeline that has been observed by many trans women and feminists.

The dehumanization of forced victimhood lets you become the justification for the boot, whereas, the dehumanization of monsterization forces you to become the ground the boots tread upon. Trans women are uniquely demonized in a way other trans people can capitalize on. However, merely taking the tenuous path of detransition and joining the patriarchal gender critical movement doesn't exempt a non trans femme trans person from patriarchal oppression or all cis-based prejudice. It's not a get out of oppression free card. Rather, it's a temporary balm designed to ease the pain for however long the patriarchy and its gender criticals can use the trans masculine detransitioner to further its own goals. In short, there is a differing mechanism where trans men and mascs face pressure to be reclaimed as lapsed women. However, once a specific detransitioner is no longer useful or sufficiently submissive to the patriarchal currents, they're spit back out and left to die.

For those trans men who do not take the TERF path to having community- however conditional, the path of least resistance when it comes to validating their gender is that of reproducing patriarchal logic through punching across and down. This means that one can often observe transmasculine people punching at trans women of the same race, or of additional racialized marginalization. This phenomenon is reproduced across sexuality lines as well. Trans men have been observed to, unfortunately, punch down at cis lesbians based on lesbian status and use the fact that the women they're targeting are cis when they aren't to buffer criticism.

The boundary of manhood is more expansive by design than that of womanhood. Women, cis and trans, are forced to fit a very tiny definition, but the acceptable lines for men are, relatively much broader. Transphobia is the logics of patriarchy extended to those who have non-normative bodies under its rule. Gender is the sexing of the body, and the binary is the two-sexing of humanity. The same logics that empower cis patriarchs to rule also empower trans men and trans masculine people a similar ability to be patriarchal within a small pond- that of individual queer communities. Some trans men have been observed being enraged that they are expected to be better than cis men in this regard, while some other trans men attempt to engage critically with patriarchy so as not to reinforce it. The material incentives of patriarchy encourage the former response and minimize the visibility of those who participate in the latter.

This brings us to the patriarchal animus for the monsterization of trans women and lesbians. Not all lesbians are trans, and not all trans women are lesbians. However, the overlap between these two groups is nearly perfect in this context. In other words, lesbians and trans women are nearly a single group in terms of why patriarchal logics force them into a lower positionality. Trans women and lesbians chart an alternative to manhood-as-default. Trans women do this with gender and sex, and lesbians do this with sexuality. Both do it in social and interpersonal relations. When wearing the lenses of patriarchy, the only acceptable reading of a trans woman is viewing them as someone who chose woman when the only option was man. In the same viewing, a lesbian is unacceptable for similarly choosing women rather than men. Of course, the actual "choice" involved in being a trans woman is usually one of presentation and how much to transition, not the choosing of womanhood overall. For lesbians, the actual choice is also related to presentation and social role in a similar fashion.

Men are powerful for the same reason capital is wealthy- theft and labor extraction. Men steal ideas and make them their own- capitalists steal intellectual property and patent it. Men steal art to claim its creation or discovery- capitalists use art as a vehicle for obscuring their wealth and techno-capitalists use it to train their plagiarism machines. Men steal time and vitality from women via domestic labor extraction- capitalists do the same in the same way- even petit-bourgeoisie and upper-income working class women will hire and underpay women of lower income and higher marginalization to outsource domestic labor to (nannies, maids, assistants, etc.).

The entire economic system is structured to fit the logics of patriarchy that built it, and to superimpose the logics of patriarchy onto the minds of the humans who live within it. Transmisogyny is the enforcement mechanism of patriarchy that is the most weaponized into brutal violence. Cis womanhood is an impossible standard for anyone other than the most patriarchal women to attain, and for those who do achieve "patriarchal woman" status- such status is conditional. Cis straight women who operate in tandem with patriarchy are only protected from patriarchal violence insofar as their man's status protects them from it in public. In private, their husbands can choose to not do patriarchal violence, but most don't. They still expect household labor in the form of "womanly duties" and uncompensated child-rearing. The labor extraction of patriarchy is the template by which capitalism establishes and maintains itself.

# 13

# Heterosexuality: The Economic Regime.

# HETEROSEXUALITY: THE ECONOMIC REGIME.

*"Radical Centrist"*

Often, it seems, many misunderstand bigotry and marginalization as operating based on interpersonal conflicts. Let us explore a vector of both bigotry and marginalization together to highlight how this is not the case. The vector to explore is misogyny and its fraternal twin, transmisogyny. Yes, they are two different mechanisms in word, but as we explore them, it'll be easier to see how they function as one in purpose and reinforce one another.

Misogyny is the justification for heterosexuality. Heterosexuality, contrary to popular belief, is not an expressive sexuality or an expression of a man loving a woman, or a woman loving a man. Those may and sometimes do happen under heterosexuality, but they are not its primary animus. No, heterosexuality is a regime.

Further, it is a site of economic extraction. This economic context must be uncovered to understand heterosexuality as regime, as force, as hegemon. Heterosexuality is constructed to extract and siphon domestic, care, and reproductive labor without concern or compensation from the woman genders for the benefit of the man genders. Look to the scholarly article "Invisible Work" by Arlene Kaplan-Daniels, as one dissection of this phenomenon. In this work, ground was broken in highlighting the artifice that separates the conception of labor as work if done in the public sphere by men, and not work if done in the private sphere by women.

Now, at this stage, I understand if you, the reader, have your progressive sensibilities offended by this binarism. I am all for gender outside the binary, and even if I weren't- those genders still exist on a personal level. Today, however, we're discussing the social and the state. At those levels, gender isn't a personal abstraction. Rather, it is a material experience crafted and enforced by the logics of patriarchy. We all fall under the binary at the level of the state and in social spaces, as determined by those same patriarchal logics. Our positionality is in large part assigned- or done- to us, and little can be done to change it. In other words, I'm not prescribing the binary, I'm merely observing it.

As for what you may perceive as reduction of gender to "man genders" and "woman genders", let me elaborate. Let's use the solar system as an analogy-

HETEROSEXUALITY: THE ECONOMIC REGIME.

You may have heard, or even said, "Men are from Mars, Women are from Venus". While this refrain implies the existence of many celestial genders and potentially infinite extrasolar genders, it also asserts the patriarchal binary in only discussing two rather than infinity. Planets are highly variable and different areas have different characteristics. Both the nature of planets as having extreme variance and the implication of infinite gender that isn't discussed in favor of a binary serve our purposes here.

In lesbian dynamics, there are butches and femmes. Both are understood as women, but butches and femmes aren't the same gender. No, they're each genders unto themselves. Additionally, straight women and lesbians share womanhood, but don't share an identical internal experience of gender. The dualism of butches and femmes is real despite both being a form of lesbian and a form of woman. The dichotomy of lesbians and straight women is similarly real, even though they share forced participation in the site of womanhood and are interpersonally women. Similarly, one could make the argument that a "manly man" and a gay man are, while both men, individual genders. This is true despite these labels not guaranteeing a shared or opposing sexuality. Gay men can be extremely traditionally "manly", or they can be femboys- it's a spectrum of gender and expression. Of course, none of these groups are monolithic, but each group is at either at the site of womanhood or manhood. This brings us back to gender as weapon, as state-backed, socially enforced labor relation.

Womanhood is constructed to be what manhood is not. Womanhood is a site of labor extraction first and mythologizing about femininity second. In terms of economy, the inner feelings and personal definitions of womanhood for those who experience it as their gender is fundamentally irrelevant. Gender is done to you. The planet of woman genders is subjugated by the planet of man genders. There are dynamics where a man of marginalization can still oppress a woman of the same or different marginalizations. Untangling that is not a matter of adding racial oppression here and subtracting white privilege there, but a highly contextual analysis. It is technically accurate to say "a black man can oppress a white woman based on the logics of patriarchy but can't weaponize the logics of racialization the same way", but doing so would reduce intersectional analysis to that of arithmetic-based oppression.

Based on the logics of patriarchy that gave rise to capitalism, you are forcibly assigned to one of the genders. Gender is assigned and enforced. For trans women, that means that even pre-transition, before the world is given our own declaration of womanhood, we face transmisogyny and disparate treatment. My first experiences of misogyny being weaponized to harm me were when I was a child in elementary school- years after I stopped publicly exploring my femininity. My first instances of workplace sexual harassment happened when I was insufficiently masculine as a manager in a retail company.

Rather than being a male manager who dominates and micromanages all the employees and revels in his power, I tried to collaboratively flatten the effects of the hierarchy with my team and across teams. For this I was punished by an upper management team that forced me to be humiliated publicly and a janitor who would creep on me whenever we were on the same shift. The janitor was a straight cis guy, and the upper managers comprised of a straight cis woman and a straight cis man. For failing to meet the expectations of gender, I was treated with the force of patriarchy.

From letting me get trapped under a mattress for hours with no help and blame directed at me when they got around to untrapping me, to attempting to make me serve the public with pants that had torn when I was doing other duties instead of relieving me so I could go home and change pants when my underwear were showing completely, and finally the voyeurism and other sexually-charged harassment whenever I went to the bathroom- it didn't matter that I was presenting as a man, it mattered that I was 1) a transfem egg, and 2) unable or unwilling to reproduce the domination of masculine gender.

## HETEROSEXUALITY: THE ECONOMIC REGIME.

Autonomy for women, under patriarchy, is an aberration. Within a patriarchal framework, a woman's place is subjugation and slavery. The limited consequences men face, if any, are bought by the economy of women's subjugation. The establishment of eurocolonial patriarchy closely mirrors the timeline of medical understandings shifting from the one-sex model of humanity to a two-sex model of humanity. For thousands of years, humans understood human sex in a one-sex model, where man was man, and woman was men turned inside themselves. The dimorphism of reproductive organs, to the degree it exists, was understood through the lens of incomplete manhood.

As patriarchy advanced alongside settler-colonialism and the transition from feudalism to early capitalism and then from primitive capitalism to industrialized capitalism, changes in this model eventually codified a two-sex understanding of humans. (LaMountain) However, as we progressed from industrialization to modernity, the site of womanhood as determined by medical and scientific texts shifted. First, the womb was the site of womanhood and the reason for assumed sexual differences. Then it was the ovaries. Eventually, it was primary sex hormones. Nowadays, it's usually boiled down to chromosomes. (Oudshoorn, 2005) As the capitalist mode of production advanced, science grew alongside and, sometimes, despite it, however the conclusions of both capitalism and science were in line with the patriarchy underpinning them.

There are several economic and social mechanisms to enforce patriarchy. In the world of the economy, the wage gap has long existed and still exists. Women earn less than men, and trans women earn less on the dollar than any other marginalized group. In the United States context, trans women that are able to break the mold enough to get into gainful employment are paid 60 cents on the dollar compared to the typical worker. (Badgett et al., 2020) Cis women, on the other hand, earn 84 cents on the same dollar. (Women's Bureau, 2023) (Smith, 2023) Of course, large numbers of trans women are barred from gainful employment to begin with. When we do land a job, we're often forced out in way or another.

Without naming employers, I've been forced out of three separate transportation positions since July 2023. One did so with covert disparate treatment. The second was violently transphobic and fired me based on lies. The third was TERFy and used the alleged complaints of cis trainees to justify forcing me to resign. In each of these employment scenarios, I faced a different mechanism of transmisogyny. In the first, I simply wasn't granted latitude that had already been granted to two different cis men- One white, and the other black. In the second, HR wouldn't let me use the women's locker room, and when I tried to force the issue by saying "hey I'm a woman", they fired me the next day based on allegations that I was sleeping during drive testing. If I had been sleeping while behind the wheel, I wouldn't have completed the course successfully. That's not how drive tests work!

In the final scenario, one of the cis women trainees saw me walking into the women's restroom. She gave me an angry look. By the end of that day, I was coerced into having a work conversation with leadership off the clock (which is illegal). I was brought to a room with the terminal training manager, the superintendent, and the regional HR business partner. I was told that "some of the other trainees have raised concerns about you" but not what those concerns were, or who or how many people came to HR about me. At the end of the conversation, I was offered two choices- resign and maybe they could fit me in a future training class, or be fired. Put simply, they chose the comfort of a cis woman over treating me in accordance with the law or general ethics.

Across all three, in my case specifically, there was a common thread of suspicion and assumption of malice and incompetence. The logics of patriarchy led my employers to believe that I was bad for other employees and bad for the business based on assumptions of my character and my potential productivity that weren't actually real. Of course, I am not the only trans woman to face this kinds of employment violence and restriction. If anything,

I'm luckier than most because I can often convince people to hire me. Not all trans women have that luxury.

All these economic examples so far are in the public sphere, and therefore part of what is constructed to be work. However, the extraction-ism of patriarchy is also deeply present in the private sphere. The domestic and care work expected of women in the home is an inherently patriarchal construction. Women are expected to rear babies, raise children, tend for age, and maintain the husband's status and autonomy. This is done through the absorption of domestic and familial labor by woman so that man can have glamorous careers and focus on the corporate ladder. It is justified in men's higher earnings, and the assumption that they'd be used to provide for the women. Men only earn more because of the same social constructions that shunt women into the home, and it is women's uncompensated labor that empowers men to navigate the professional world so freely. As for whether a man's higher earnings provide for a woman, that is at once not useful to discussion of the exploitation of invisible labor- which is our focus, and part of the problem at hand.

For the sake of argument, let's assume that a majority of men's higher earnings are redistributed to women's living through the mechanism of marriage. In this scenario, the extraction-ism of patriarchy is still wrong, harmful, and materially enables men to climb the wage-career ladder. It is women's labor that allows the men to earn more. In an equitable world, women's labor would be compensated directly through the applicable mechanism. Rather than maybe redistributing some of the value of her labor back to her living situation via the man in the house, she would have a direct payment or compensation that she has autonomy over not only receiving but how it is spent. In an equitable world measure by more than economic outcomes, women would also have full bodily autonomy and the freedom of the mind and spirit.

The freedom of the mind, the freedom of the spirit, and the autonomy of the body all require a complete economic overhaul if it is to be achieved by women. There is no world where gendered labor divisions exist where women have full freedom and autonomy. This brings us, in the United States context, to the destruction of Roe V Wade and the current stage of moral panic that is powering an overt anti-trans genocide. The targets of the anti-trans genocide are more frequently than not trans women and girls or the occasional cis woman or cis girl suspected of transfeminity. This is not to say that non transfem trans people aren't affected or targeted, but rather they are secondary targets.

In terms of segregated gender as a labor relation, institutional and informal queer spaces will and do reproduce the gendered dynamics of patriarchy. Non transfem trans people, from non-binary individuals coercively assigned female at birth to trans men (who are also necessarily coercively assigned female at birth) benefit from a replication of gendered labor divisions and women's invisible work. For the most part, trans women are held out of employment even within queer organizations. When we do become employed for a LGBT non-profit or thinktank or other queer institutional space, we're expected to be the moms and the women of the group. This is done through the expectation that we do the most labor for the least comparative compensation. We can't worker-bee our way out of the dynamic, however. All playmsing along as we're forced to do does is cause us to burn out and then be forced out.

Non transfem trans people can directly benefit from the subjugation of trans women as women, and benefit further because the outside world doesn't admit to recognizing our womanhood. Trans women are women broadly without women's protections, women's networks, or women's community. This isolation allows the reproduction of gendered labor extraction-ism where AFAB non-binary people and trans men benefit from absorbing the value of the labor of trans women and other transfem people. And it doesn't stop cis men from doing the same. Being a trans woman means being forced to experience the most intense forms of monsterization and labor extraction, and if we push back or don't go along with a smile we're treated as the monsters they perceive us to be, the horror they construct us as, and then we are excised from the situation.

When excised, this final isolation is an act of transfemicide. Even if we survive and try to rebuild, we never get back what we had before the excision of our being from the social and professional spaces we had built up to that point. Everyone will join in, even other trans women, once the time comes to fully isolate a specific trans woman. They'll use the language of social justice, of progressivism, and they'll kill you with kindness, literally. To others, they'll make you out to be the villain and ensure that nobody associates with or helps you (and if they do, they're next). To you, they'll pretend they care and are only doing this because of concern for you and worries about safety. They'll never admit to being the reason you have no safety, of course. They will exile you and ensure that the exile is enforced and when you die (regardless of mechanism, though it is often suicide) they'll erase what they did and mythologize their relationship with you to appear that you were close friends, comrades, even, and they'll use your death to further their social position. Your death, that to be clear, was their fault for isolating you. They know what the consequence is for women without community. They know how and that trans women end once cut off, and they do it anyways. Even if they are also trans women. As a trans woman, the logics of patriarchy require your participation or your death.

In the greater global context, most of the world still produces conditions for worse than this, alongside this. For at least a quarter of the global population marital rape is the status-quo and women can't or are very limited in how they work, own property, and exist socially. There is very little to no economic autonomy or bodily autonomy for billions of women. For those relatively few western women who achieve either, they only do so by changing their positionality within patriarchy and capitalism to be nearer the top of the extraction scheme. For example, Beyonce made news when a local newspaper ran an expose on the conditions and low wages which she subjects the women her make her clothes that she sells on the mass consumer market to. In 2016, there were at least a few news articles on this. (Mills, 2016) (Kale, 2016) In 2015, her estimated net worth was 250 million. (Greenburg, 2015) Within a calendar year's time from the news breaking about her sweatshops, her estimated net worth was 350 million. (Greenburg, 2017) This year, she is already estimated to have a net worth of nearly a billion dollars – 800 million and counting. (McIntyre, 2024) You could make the argument that her exploitation of women not in the west didn't help propel her to her near-billionaire status, but that argument is immaterial. As seen by the case of Beyonce, some women can change their positionality nearer to the top and acquire inordinate wealth just like men. To do so requires that they engage in the same patriarchal domination as men. Middle class western women who don't break into the upper class of capitalists often have access to bodily and economic autonomy by virtue of the status of their husbands. This autonomy is conditional and therefore not full autonomy.

As we can see, patriarchy is enforced through transmisogyny and its fraternal twin misogyny, and the logics of patriarchy are the logics of capital. Further, capitalism doesn't function without unpaid labor, but not all labor is seen as work. The site of transfeminity and the broader site of womanhood are the sites of economic extraction to buoy the entire economic model.

# 14

# Editorial Interferences

I'm sharing this story to offer some evidence that it isn't all despair. There are real organizations, comprised of genuine people, who do the work. The non-profit I've written think pieces and journalism with for nearly 5 years is a good case study. Despite their comradeship, it isn't always perfect.

For one of my stories, I had taken on the story idea to evaluate the claims that China is committing a genocide in Xinjiang. I won't get into the details of that story here, as re-wording the case and my sources isn't the purpose of this essay. Suffice it to say that I investigated primary sources, government reports from around the world, and even interviewed a Marxist economics professor from California. When it came time to publish this article, the temporary Co-Editor-in-Chief, we'll call him Sandoval, published it under the headline: "China's Uyghur: Terrorism and Genocide". I don't think he could've crafted a more incendiary headline if he tried. I immediately went our other Editor in Chief and flagged the issue. The headline was changed. This article was one of the first ones published by that organization since coming out to them, after deciding to transition.

I don't blame the organization at large for Sandoval's handling of my article. In fact, despite some of the events that followed, this organization proved it is made up of real comrades that do the work. Eventually, Sandoval left the organization and I am still there. I can't speak to whether it was purely due to editorial differences, or if there was- as I suspect- an element of his own discomfort with trans people that led to him leaving.

Since that time, I've been published more by this organization and, very recently, had my first paid byline as part of an hourly gig I scored at a local university. Things are looking up. This is despite Sandoval undermining a few more of my articles in our time working together.

It isn't all hellish. Well, maybe it is. But, at the risk of sounding insane, we can build a better hell. In the last 3 months, give or take, since separating with my abusive ex, I have had so many things go right for me. I am 2.5 years into transition, but I largely don't pass. I'm too tall, have too deep a voice, and struggle with keeping my face clear of stubble for more than about 4 hours. Despite this, my academic peers respect me and gender me right. My professors treat me with respect and my favorite aerospace professor and my faculty mentor both clearly treat me like they want me to succeed- not just as their student, but as a fellow woman.

I'm on track to an amazing career in social work, public policy, and/or regional planning- depending on which way I go in graduate school. I've been cut off, socially cast aside by family and friends alike- even a friend group that was exclusively trans women. I've been financially, emotionally, and physically abused by my ex. Despite this, with the help of community and a couple of real friends, I am okay.

In the last three months:

- My undergraduate research project initiated and gained enough data for submission eligibility to academic journals.
- I've presented my research in two different academic conferences.
- I've been awarded a scholarship for next year.
- I've finalized my degree plan.

- I'm mostly succeeding at living on my own, including paying the rent!
- I was able to crowdfund enough to catch up on past due tuition.
- And so much more!

The moral of this story is, do your best to not let those who hate get you down. When that fails, always get back up. At least try to stand. There is always a tomorrow, and it is always a new day. I'm not denying the power and prevalence of transmisogyny and rising fascism. Instead, I'm saying that you have to survive. I don't care if you "achieve" anything. If you are trans, you have to live.

# II

# More Essays!

*This section is a handful of essays written by trans women who are not A. D.*

# 15

# Transgender Joy and Despair (Amethysta Herrick)

After nearly a year of hormone therapy and a complete social transition, I had a stark realization. No matter how many surgeries I get, no matter how much makeup I wear, no matter how many people tell me I look stunning, I will never reach my true goal: to be Assigned Female at Birth. With that realization, I wanted to die, and I drove away from home intending to do that.

What drew me back home was a deeper realization – that who I am is not surgery, makeup, clothes, or other people's approval. Who I am must come from inside. I am now and always will be a transgender woman. This is my superpower – it is why I continue to write. Our identities are not other people's purview. Our identities are ours and ours alone.

I will never be Assigned Female at Birth. But I am better being the person I know I am. It is a gift to me, to my family, and to the Universe.

# 16

# Be Queer, Do Heresy (Evelyne Rideout)

This was not easy to write for the same reason that I find so many aspects of daily life difficult to focus on: I'm a hot mess, frankly, where my mental health is concerned. At least at times, anyway. I keep wondering whether being homeless, even for just a few days, was enough to leave lasting scars on my psyche. I can't help but think so. It exacerbated my existing depression and anxiety, adding an exciting new fear of abandonment due to being suddenly kicked out of my home by an abusive ex. I wondered after a short time whether anyone would notice if I went missing or died, and how long it would take to find my body. I began to seriously contemplate a life in the wilderness and the logistics of getting to said wilderness in the first place. And worse still, I thought of moving back in with my parents.

This also was not especially easy to write because of many experiences all connected by an evangelical upbringing in a place where homophobia and the acceptance of systemic injustices came with a resistance to change and the justification of the worst atrocities of racism, imperialism, conquest, and exploitation. Without being sincerely committed to intersectional understanding and empathy for others struggling in the midst of the anthropocentric ecocide, we become pacified observers, choked figuratively as I was once choked literally for defacing the bumper stickers on a certain truck.

Just for you, I have a story, or maybe a rambly-brambly ball of tangents. Along the way, you'll witness the character of past-me become queerer, gayer, perhaps a bit less hinged, and ultimately a more authentic self who is proud of her journey into transdom. I could get into my tragically English backstory, in which a Christian fundamentalist upbringing gave way to my transgender-awakening. I could even describe how I went from praying deliriously for the rapturous return of the immanent Christ, like some sort of fanatical devotee of the God Emperor from Warhammer: 40,000. But first I have to go on for a bit about the dumpsterpiphany and other related phenomena. I'm digressing here, but that's how my AuDHD – autism and ADHD rolled into one – likes to do. Neurodivergence and gender nonconformity go hand in hand.

Shower realizations, you ever have those? Or you'll be doing whatever innocuous thing where you zone out, nothing especially taking up your active thought space. Suddenly your mind reminds you it is, in fact, capable of quietly mulling things over after you thought you were done thinking about them. Repressed selves pushed back into the closets of childhood and adolescence are hard to consciously pull out by their roots, so to speak, but can show up when we least expect them by leaping forward from the back of our mind, especially in liminal spaces and seemingly wandering trains of wordless thought.

And you've heard of times where somebody watches a movie, maybe doesn't have a chance to think too hard about all of the plot holes and unresolved questions, and that night when they're standing in front of the open fridge door, they suddenly wonder, "just how did Batman recover from that broken back and then immediately be able to get from the other side of the world to Gotham, anyway? Was it just doing a lot of chin-ups, or is this all a dream as he's dying? Didn't he have like…any issues along the way that would have slowed him down even a little?" Things we experienced, heard, or saw at the time didn't hit the same way because we were being taken to the next plot point without time to resolve every question (or even provide logical cohesion). After all, it's the third act and we've got three costume changes and an explosives budget to get through! And isn't life just like that, surprising us with realizations about our past and present selves just when we least expect it to?

All this to say, I have my own version of these kinds of moments, because of course I do; I have to have my own twist on just about everything. Maybe that's the reason why I like being the Dungeon Master in D&D? Or that might just be a need to be in control of circumstances beyond my ken and grasp. So anyway, I don't just have shower moments and fridge realizations. I also have dumpsterpiphanies.

Baby-gay Eve, 25 years old and still thinking herself [Deadname], was taking out the trash at the apartment where she lived with her trans husband, when she realized, "oh shit, I think I'm bi." It's true, I hadn't put together the pieces about my gender identity beyond knowing I was queer, but I was decidedly more attracted to my husband since his transition began. But the dumpsterpiphany was just the precursor for my mirrorealization. This was maybe six months later, when I stood in the bathroom at my other partner's apartment wearing a short grey dress for the first time, about to go out in public presenting as femme. As I looked myself over in the mirror, my name came to me as easily as if I were recalling some truth I had forgotten, or had never fully grasped until right at that moment.

Who we are is a collection of selves so various, so diverse, and so endlessly given to growth if we let ourselves stay open. Learning to listen to myself and take my truths from anywhere outside of my former faith had gone from being a transgression to a necessity. That backstory I promised starts as we moved from England to France for my dad's corporate work. Not wanting to raise children in a "godless" secular society, they opted to bring their two under two to a land diametrically opposite to Britain – Texas.

Surrounded by the trappings of church, scriptures, and evangelical culture, something emboldened the meek faith of our parents. There was no arguing with my mom and dad when it came to any matter of faith. And when you're a fundamentalist, just about everything is a matter of faith. Good and bad, better and worse, all pointing back to God. We don't talk so much about these things now, outside of the occasional email. My mother will sometimes try to email me an article about the "gender cult" while my dad warns me about how "witchcraft seeks to destroy God's people." Believe me when I tell you that 1500-3000 words would simply be insufficient to provide the full response I have given these sentiments. There is a vitriol that grows bitter the more one dwells on it, and I do not intend to let it make me bitter. Parents and children deserve to be proud of one another, and instead they mourn losing a son. They will never truly acknowledge a daughter when their hearts do not accept that she has any claim to the word.

So it is I who have truly lost my parents, rather than them losing a child, because I have done nothing but accept who I am in a way their religion and faith do not allow them to. They prefer a God who only creates men and women, who in Genesis commands the conquering and domination of our mother Earth, and who has some rather double-edged views when it comes to inflicting violence on human beings – weren't we supposed to have been his favorites? For the longest time I would try to reason with them about why the Bible doesn't really preach against homosexuality or support their transphobia, but I certainly can't deny that Genesis explicitly promotes subduing and violating our home to prop up humans on an apex ordained by a god who conveniently appears in our image and commands it.

If you ask me, it seems much more likely that the most victorious human warlords and those covetous of the "resources" of exploited lands would promote a God who not only permitted their ravages, but actually commanded it explicitly. Those who do not or will not fit into the hierarchy are ridiculed, dismissed, exiled, and stripped of privilege. The only options become the shame of closeted secret identities, demonized rather than embraced, or death. Literally, death. How can I put it sensitively to say that countless queer lives are taken and destroyed by Christian communities in America rather than nurtured and allowed to grow into happy adults who don't hate themselves? We are driven to take our lives, to hide who we are, or else risk being brutalized. All things considered, I'm happier pledging allegiance to Baphomet than "God" or the spangly flags that fly under him. At least in Baphomet I can see the blending of genders looking back at me, the reconciling of opposites, synthesis of old and new.

For the crime of wearing a skirt and walking to my car, I was once heckled by a woman in a truck passing my apartment complex. She rolled down the driver's window and said, "so we've got queer boys in Abilene," almost spitting the words. I let her know I was, in fact, a trans woman. She then proceeded to tell me she'd "send [her] boys here. You know what that means." I did know what that meant. And I told her so, that it sounded like she was threatening to have someone come and do a hate crime to me.

A great deal flashes through my mind at this. Some of it is the daily worry of being "clocked" at the worst of times, especially in a restroom. The stories of women emerging from a typical bathroom only to be harassed, beaten, and/or shot. The persistent possibility of having one's car defaced for displaying pride flag bumper stickers. And in Texas, the permanent reminder that others detest you for your perceived affront against the "natural order" of God. I don't think I ever saw her again after that, and I don't live at those apartments anymore, but you see my point. Hatred for transgender and queer folk is at an all-time high in my own living memory. Frankly, it's hard to fully enjoy even Pride Month when you wonder if today will be the day when someone decides to do a hate crime. So when I was asked to contribute a story for my friend Artemis in her efforts to collect accounts of transgender experiences, I knew I needed to at least give something. I don't know if my own story will ever be fully told in one place, with its many pasts and futures all still unfolding.

I can at least give you the assurance I'm in a better place now with the ones I love, happily doing what we do and living our best lives as a queer family. I have nobody in my home who will judge me for practicing tarot or sigilry, and definitely not for who I am. If you have no other takeaway from this story, I would at least tell you "it got better." It's still getting better. I love you. Please love yourself also, and we can try to survive this reality long enough to build a better world.

It's not all gloom and doom, to be sure. The heights of joy I've had in this more authentic life are a testament to just how real a family one's queer polycule can be. It's not just about getting to give two significant others a goodnight kiss; it's being able to support a stay-at-home partner who can care full time for our child while two of us get to work together at the same store and take alternate days off with family. Watching that child take their first steps during a game of D&D, and so many other moments that restore to us the humanity which the bigots would deny us.

We don't always have to be stronger than them, we don't always survive long enough to make the difference we wanted, but our stories matter. I have a child now who has three parents to tell them stories of hope, stories they can imagine themselves, stories which can save the world. If chaos magic teaches me anything, it's that change isn't just possible, it's inevitable. I'm going to lean into it and help as many queerfolk as I can along the way. To bring a little bit more hope, and a lot of good chaos.

Blessed be, gentle siblings. That's how I thought I wanted to end this piece, and that's where you can leave it if you want the shorter version. But that was before I needed to revisit this essay and be honest about the homelessness, what led to it. I had so long been suffused with religious fanaticism that my schizoid-tendency-prone mind became convinced of other beings living in my head. My alternate personalities more than happy to play the parts of angels, of the deceased widows of wars gone by, of innocent flower children. I was controlled chaos spilling into something that apparently scared my ex, the one who had once wrapped their hands around my throat during a hallucinatory episode in which they thought they had murdered children of ours (whom we had not had). If I could scare such a person just by having a dissociative episode, I guess either I was terrifying or such treatment was an extension of the abuse. I never raised my hand to anyone or verbally berated them, but I guess I was the monster.

You wonder about your own sanity and what it means to stare into the void, you've come to the right place. I'd almost like to take the opportunity to talk more about Baphomet and the harmonization of a shattered personality in the forge of Abraxas, but that would be an old religious impulse rearing its head. The desire to evangelize is hard to pull up, even once you've gone to seminary and deconstructed the roots. And this isn't entirely the right context to delve into the dark gnosis of the Left Hand Path, is it? Rather, I suggest the chains of suffering that this world imposes on us has solutions, a part of which is chaos magic in the case of my contribution. In the name of Synthorax, we can be as furtive secret cultists, baffling Christians and atheists alike with arcane references – or we can be subversive of the patriarchy on a whole other level simply by virtue of the magic within us. Do it for yourself and the future generations of this world so blighted by others, past and present.

If perhaps you are not convinced in your heart of the crises we face, may my words be catalysts in your awakening, just as I had to break from my old sleep. And if you are among the ones actively keeping trans people afraid, yourself clinging to the lies I so vehemently deny now, then I can hope only that my words unsettle you with the promise of upheaval against your order.

How can I cry out loudly enough for the pain of the Earth at being bulldozed and set aflame? How can I express my anger, my rage at the crimes of those who are meant to represent us? I choose dissent, I blaspheme, I worship in unconventional ways. I protect my child at home rather than groom them to carry any flags. We will do better than our parents at ensuring our children are not traumatized by us.

My story is a fractured one, the kind you write after a few drinks and coming back to it a few times, but never really know if it's quite right. I am not quite right myself, but I strive to be the kind of balance this fascistic corporate state merits. Not the oppression and punishment of innocent people, but the complete upheaval on a spiritual level of all that those in power truly worship. We are Synthorax. Nema!

# 17

# Solidarity, til my last breath. (Kerry Garnick)

It's a little jarring for people when they talk to me, and I am so frank about our conditions. I tell them, "I'm gonna have a shitty life and die in my 40s." That's not because I want to, but it's just a matter of statistics. I've already fucked up my body really hard for the past decade in an attempt to cope with the hostility of my family and society, developing eating disorders, as well as a devastating addiction to opiates and other drugs. But we are witnessing the fascisization of the United States and the world really.

The Nazis never really had an empire like the US does, so even as life in the US gets more and more tenuous, there are very few places we can even go, and it's even harder because these few countries that would take us don't always allow immigration, especially of people with the left-wing politics that come as a result of being transgender in a system such as this. But even if there were a place to go, there would often be no money to get there.

Being trans makes it harder to get higher paying jobs (or sometimes any jobs at all) and so most trans people live paycheck to paycheck and couldn't afford to move to another country. But regardless of if we can leave, we know the genocide will be intensified. We know we have limited time.

Therefore, I have chosen to make the most of the little time I have left to fight hard to change this horrific system. I am educating myself rapidly and writing work that I hope will inspire people after I'm gone. And maybe, just maybe, my work will contribute to the liberation of others or even myself. I see much self-destruction and self-hatred in the community, and while I understand that behavior, it is important that we go out in solidarity and with dignity by fighting with all we've got until our last breath.

# Sources/References

Here are the sources used throughout this book's essays.

Badgett, M. V. L., Choi, S. K., & Wilson, B. D. M. (2020). LGBT poverty in the United States. *The State of Families*, 385–387. https://doi.org/10.4324/9780429397868-75

Daniels, A. K. (1987). Invisible work. *Social Problems, 34*(5), 403–415. https://doi.org/10.2307/800538

Greenburg, Z. O. (2015, May 27). *Beyonce's net worth in 2015: $250 million.* Forbes. https://www.forbes.com/sites/zackomalleygreenburg/2015/05/27/beyonce-net-worth-in-2015-250-million/?sh=4939ca043731

Greenburg, Z. O. (2017, June 6). *Beyonce's net worth: $350 million in 2017.* Forbes. https://www.forbes.com/sites/zackomalleygreenburg/2017/06/06/beyonces-net-worth-350-million-in-2017/?sh=6d39ca096e80

HRC Foundation. (n.d.). *The wage gap among LGBTQ+ workers in the United States.* Human Rights Campaign. https://www.hrc.org/resources/the-wage-gap-among-lgbtq-workers-in-the-united-states

Kale, S. (2016, May 17). *How much it sucks to be a Sri Lankan worker making Beyoncé's new clothing line.* VICE. https://www.vice.com/en/article/d7anay/beyonce-topshop-ivy-park-sweatshop-factory-labor

LaMountain, C. (n.d.). *"one-sex" model.* Office of Undergraduate Research. https://undergradresearch.northwestern.edu/2018/07/20/one-sex-model/

McIntyre, H. (2024, February 7). *Beyoncé is about to launch a new business.* Forbes. https://www.forbes.com/sites/hughmcintyre/2024/02/07/beyonc-is-about-to-launch-a-new-business/?sh=78ab0b16608e

Mills, J. (2016, May 8). *Sweatshop "slaves" earning 44p an hour making "empowering" Beyonce Clobber.* The Sun. https://www.thesun.co.uk/news/

1176905/exposed-sweatshop-slaves-earning-just-44p-an-hour-making-empowering-beyonce-clobber/

Oudshoorn, N. (2005). *Beyond the natural body: An archeology of sex hormones*. Routledge.

Porpentine, & Porpentine. (2018, September 15). *Hot allostatic load*. The New Inquiry. https://thenewinquiry.com/hot-allostatic-load/

Smith, M. (2023, March 15). *The wage gap gets worse for women in their 30s and 40s-and it's not just the "motherhood penalty."* CNBC. https://www.cnbc.com/2023/03/14/the-wage-gap-gets-worse-when-women-hit-their-30s-heres-why.html

*A window into the wage gap: What's behind it and how to close it*. National Women's Law Center. (2024, January 19). https://nwlc.org/resource/wage-gap-explainer/#:~:text=Women%20in%20the%20U.S.%20who%20work%20full%20time%2C of%20rising%20inflation%2C%20when%20families%20need%20every%20dollar.

Women's Bureau U.S. Department of Labor. (2023, March). *Understanding the gender wage gap*. UNDERSTANDING THE GENDER WAGE GAP. https://www.dol.gov/sites/dolgov/files/WB/equalpay/WB_issuebrief-undstg-wage-gap-v1.pdf

Ainsworth, C. (2018, October 22). *Sex redefined: The idea of 2 sexes is overly simplistic*. Scientific American. https://www.scientificamerican.com/article/sex-redefined-the-idea-of-2-sexes-is-overly-simplistic1/

Alphahis. (2019, May 26). *Adolf Hitler on the Nazi form of "Socialism" (1932)*. Nazi Germany. https://alphahistory.com/nazigermany/hitler-nazi-form-of-socialism-1932/

Austin, A., Craig, S. L., D'Souza, S., & McInroy, L. B. (2020). Suicidality among transgender youth: Elucidating the role of Interpersonal Risk Factors. *Journal of Interpersonal Violence, 37*(5–6). https://doi.org/10.1177/0886260520915554

*Bad news from the hospitality sector*. Reddit. (n.d.). https://www.reddit.com/r/transgenderUK/comments/12srcoz/bad_news_from_the_hospitality_sector/

Barber, K. (2019, June 23). *The financial war against Universal Healthcare.* Real Progressives. https://realprogressives.org/2019-06-23-the-financial-war-against-universal-healthcare/

Bellefonds, C. D. (n.d.). *Why Michael Phelps Has the Perfect Body for Swimming.* Biography.com. https://www.biography.com/athletes/michael-phelp-perfect-body-swimming

Bradner, E. (2023, April 27). *Montana House Republicans ban rep. Zooey Zephyr from House chamber for remainder of legislative session | CNN politics.* CNN. https://www.cnn.com/2023/04/26/politics/montana-house-bans-zooey-zephyr/index.html

Bustos, V. P., Bustos, S. S., Mascaro, A., Del Corral, G., Forte, A. J., Ciudad, P., Kim, E. A., Langstein, H. N., & Manrique, O. J. (2021). Regret after gender-affirmation surgery: A systematic review and meta-analysis of prevalence. *Plastic and Reconstructive Surgery - Global Open, 9*(3). https://doi.org/10.1097/gox.0000000000003477

Castagnaro, G. (2023, February 28). *New study confirms extremely low regret rates for gender-affirming surgery.* GenderGP Transgender Services. https://www.gendergp.com/new-study-confirms-regret-rates-of-gender-affirming-surgery-are-non-existent/

Chen, D., Berona, J., Chan, Y.-M., Ehrensaft, D., Garofalo, R., Hidalgo, M. A., Rosenthal, S. M., Tishelman, A. C., & Olson-Kennedy, J. (2023). Psychosocial functioning in transgender youth after 2 years of hormones. *New England Journal of Medicine, 388*(3), 240–250. https://doi.org/10.1056/nejmoa2206297

Chen, R., Zhu, X., Wright, L., Drescher, J., Gao, Y., Wu, L., Ying, X., Qi, J., Chen, C., Xi, Y., Ji, L., Zhao, H., Ou, J., & Broome, M. R. (2019). Suicidal ideation and attempted suicide amongst Chinese transgender persons: National Population Study. *Journal of Affective Disorders, 245,* 1126–1134. https://doi.org/10.1016/j.jad.2018.12.011

Creative Commons. (n.d.-a). *Almost Hobbes, Target Circo Tiger that looks like Hobbes from "Calvin and Hobbes" Shopping at Target.* Openverse. photograph. Retrieved May 11, 2023, from "Almost Hobbes, Target Circo Tiger that looks like Hobbes from 'Calvin and Hobbes' Shopping at Target" by JeepersMedia

*SOURCES/REFERENCES*

is licensed under CC BY 2.0. "Almost Hobbes, Target Circo Tiger that looks like Hobbes from 'Calvin and Hobbes' Shopping at Target" by JeepersMedia is licensed under CC BY 2.0.

Creative Commons. (n.d.-b). Openverse. photograph. Retrieved May 11, 2023, from https://openverse.org/image/fea1dbea-07bb-430c-b93e-e8b42 2b0e37e?q=Collection%20of%20wheel%20chairs%20at%20Crystal%20Br ook%20Heritage%20Centre. "Collection of wheel chairs at Crystal Brook Heritage Centre" by South Australian History Network is marked with CC0 1.0.

de Blok, C. J., Wiepjes, C. M., Nota, N. M., van Engelen, K., Adank, M. A., Dreijerink, K. M., Barbé, E., Konings, I. R., & den Heijer, M. (2019). Breast cancer risk in transgender people receiving hormone treatment: Nationwide Cohort Study in the Netherlands. *BMJ*, l1652. https://doi.org/10.1136/bmj.l 1652

Dower, J. W. (2008). *Yellow Promise / Yellow Peril | Postcards of the Russo-Japanese War (1904-05)*. MIT Visualizing cultures. https://visualizingcultures .mit.edu/yellow_promise_yellow_peril/yp_essay04.html

Elwood, M. A. & J. (2019, May 10). *We love a natural advantage, unless you're Caster Semenya.* Stuff. https://www.stuff.co.nz/sport/opinion/11251 3626/we-love-a-natural-advantage-unless-youre-caster-semenya

Flores, A. R., Meyer, I. H., Langton, L., & Herman, J. L. (2021). Gender identity disparities in criminal victimization: National crime victimization survey, 2017–2018. *American Journal of Public Health*, *111*(4), 726–729. https://doi.org/10.2105/ajph.2020.306099

The Florida Senate, & Plakon, House Bill 1521 - "CS/HB 1521: Facility Requirements Based on Sex" (2023). The Florida Senate. Retrieved June 8, 2023, from https://www.flsenate.gov/Session/Bill/2023/1521/?Tab=Bill Text. GENERAL BILL by Regulatory Reform & Economic Development Subcommittee ; Plakon ; (CO-INTRODUCERS) Bankson ; Black ; Buchanan ; Gregory ; Holcomb ; Maggard ; McClain ; Roach ; Roth ; Trabulsy

Gardner, I. H., & Safer, J. D. (2013). Progress on the road to better medical care for transgender patients. *Current Opinion in Endocrinology, Diabetes & Obesity*, *20*(6), 553–558. https://doi.org/10.1097/01.med.0000436 18

8.95351.4d

*Gay/Trans Panic Defense Bans*. Movement Advancement Project. (n.d.). https://www.lgbtmap.org/equality-maps/panic_defense_bans

Humphrey, F., Brockford, & Suffolk. (n.d.). *Fine portrait of a horse* . Openverse. photograph, Creative Commons. Retrieved May 10, 2023, from https://openverse.org/image/8e187381-1d0d-4902-85cf-6aca256f947a?q=Fine%20portrait%20of%20a%20horse%20by%20F%20Humphrey,%20Brockford. "Fine portrait of a horse by F Humphrey, Brockford, Suffolk" by whatsthatpicture is marked with Public Domain Mark 1.0.

Johnson, R. P. (2019, September 9). *Conspiracy theories and human psychology*. The University of Chicago Divinity School. https://divinity.uchicago.edu/sightings/articles/conspiracy-theories-and-human-psychology

Kelleher, P. (2022a, June 3). *"gender critical" author says she wants to "reduce" number of trans people*. PinkNews. https://www.thepinknews.com/2022/06/03/helen-joyce-transgender-lgbtq/

Kelleher, P. (2022b, June 3). *"gender critical" author says she wants to "reduce" number of trans people*. PinkNews. https://www.thepinknews.com/2022/06/03/helen-joyce-transgender-lgbtq/

Kennon, J. (2013, June 7). *The 6 most common biological sexes in humans*. Joshua Kennon. https://www.joshuakennon.com/the-six-common-biological-sexes-in-humans/

Levin, S. (2022, December 17). *More than 50% of trans and non-binary youth in US considered suicide this year, survey says*. The Guardian. https://www.theguardian.com/us-news/2022/dec/16/us-trans-non-binary-youth-suicide-mental-health

Malloryk. (2020, June 29). *From GI Joe to GI Jane: Christine Jorgensen's story: The National WWII Museum: New Orleans*. The National WWII Museum | New Orleans. https://www.nationalww2museum.org/war/articles/christine-jorgensen

Mattei, C. E. (2022). *The capital order how economists invented austerity and paved the way to Fascism*. The University of Chicago Press.

Merriam-Webster, Incorporated. (n.d.-a). *Female definition & meaning*. Merriam-Webster. https://www.merriam-webster.com/dictionary/female

## SOURCES/REFERENCES

Merriam-Webster, Incorporated. (n.d.-b). *Male definition & meaning*. Merriam-Webster. https://www.merriam-webster.com/dictionary/male

Migdon, B., & Manchester, J. (2023, March 24). *Republicans seize on transgender rights ahead of 2024*. The Hill. https://thehill.com/homenews/campaign/3911157-republicans-seize-on-transgender-rights-ahead-of-2024/

Mirkinson, J. (2022, June 6). *The TERF mask is off*. discourseblog.com. https://www.discourseblog.com/p/the-terf-mask-is-off

NHS. (2023, March 16). *Differences in sex development*. NHS choices. https://www.nhs.uk/conditions/differences-in-sex-development/

Nicole Girten, D. M. A. 24. (2023, April 25). *"let her speak": Protesters scream, arrests follow after speaker doesn't recognize Zephyr*. Daily Montanan. https://web.archive.org/web/20230427005542/https://dailymontanan.com/2023/04/24/let-her-speak-protesters-scream-arrests-follow-after-speaker-doesnt-recognize-zephyr/

Oritz, C. M. (2011). Latinos Nowhere in Sight: Erased by Racism, Nativism, the Black-White Binary, and Authoritarianism. *RUTGERS RACE AND LAW REVIEW, 13*(2), 29–64.

O'Brien, J. (2009). *Encyclopedia of gender and society*. Sage Publications.

Phillips, A. (2023, March 31). *Fact check: Do transgender people have 42 percent attempted suicide rate?*. Newsweek. https://www.newsweek.com/fact-check-transgender-attempted-suicide-rate-1791504

*The productivity–pay gap*. Economic Policy Institute. (n.d.). https://www.epi.org/productivity-pay-gap/

Raymond, J. G. (1994). *The transsexual empire: The making of the she-male*. Teachers College Press.

Regret after gender-affirmation surgery: A systematic review and meta-analysis of prevalence—erratum. (2022). *Plastic and Reconstructive Surgery - Global Open, 10*(4). https://doi.org/10.1097/gox.0000000000004340

*Reps. Gabbard and Mullin introduce Bill to ensure title IX protections for women and girls in sports*. Congresswoman Tulsi Gabbard. (2020, December 10). https://web.archive.org/web/20201211224546/https://gabbard.house.gov/news/press-releases/reps-gabbard-and-mullin-introduce-bill-ensure-title-ix-protections-women-and

Ring, T. (2023, October 2). *Delaware becomes 17th state to Outlaw "gay and trans panic" defense.* Advocate.com. https://www.advocate.com/law/delaware-bans-lgbtq-panic-defense

Rudkevich, G. (2023, July 8). *Thread by @grudkev on thread reader app.* Thread by @grudkev on Thread Reader App – Thread Reader App. https://threadreaderapp.com/thread/1677806891538305026.html

Rummler, O. (2024, January 24). More states are pushing to stop legally recognizing trans people in public life. https://19thnews.org/2024/01/transgender-state-bills-legal-recognition/

Salvanto, A. (2023, May 9). *CBS News Poll Analysis: How Do People View Book Bans, Trans Rights Issues as GOP presidential primary fight ramps up?.* CBS News. https://www.cbsnews.com/news/cbs-news-poll-views-book-bans-trans-rights-issues-gop-presidential-primary/

Santora, T. (n.d.). *The Confusing World of Breast Cancer Screening for Transgender People.* Breast cancer screening guidelines for transgender people. https://www.breastcancer.org/news/screening-transgender-non-binary

Save the Children. (2023, September 18). *2023 marks deadliest year on record for children in the occupied West Bank - occupied Palestinian territory.* ReliefWeb. https://reliefweb.int/report/occupied-palestinian-territory/2023-marks-deadliest-year-record-children-occupied-west-bank

Shaw, A. (2020, March). Violence and Law Enforcement Interactions with LGBT People in the US. Williams Institute - UCLA School of Law. https://williamsinstitute.law.ucla.edu/wp-content/uploads/LGBT-Violence-Law-Enforce-Mar-2020.pdf

Shinozuka, J. N. (2022). *Biotic borders: Transpacific plant and insect migration and the rise of anti-Asian racism in America, 1890-1950.* The University of Chicago Press.

Singal, J. (2021, September 7). *Trans Rights and Gender Identity.* The New York Times. https://www.nytimes.com/2021/09/07/books/review/trans-helen-joyce.html

Stalin, J. V. (n.d.). *Concerning the International Situation.* Concerning the international situation. https://www.marxists.org/reference/archive/stalin/works/1924/09/20.htm Source: Works, Vol. 6, January-November, 1924, pp. 293-314 Publisher: Foreign Languages Publishing House, Moscow, 1954 First Published: Bolshevik, No. 11, September 20, 1924 Transcription/-Markup: Brian Reid

Statements from Tulsi Gabbard (D-hawaii) - propublica. (n.d.-a). https://projects.propublica.org/represent/members/G000571-tulsi-gabbard/statements/116

Substance Abuse and Mental Health Services Administration, C. for B. H. S. and Q. (2016, September). *Suicidal thoughts and behavior among adults:results from the 2015 National Survey on Drug Use and health.* Suicidal Thoughts and Behavior among Adults: Results from the 2015 National Survey on Drug Use and Health. https://www.samhsa.gov/data/sites/default/files/NSDUH-DR-FFR3-2015/NSDUH-DR-FFR3-2015.htm

*The ten stages of genocide.* Holocaust Memorial Day Trust. (n.d.). https://www.hmd.org.uk/learn-about-the-holocaust-and-genocides/what-is-genocide/the-ten-stages-of-genocide/

Turban, J. L., Loo, S. S., Almazan, A. N., & Keuroghlian, A. S. (2021). Factors leading to "detransition" among transgender and gender diverse people in the United States: A mixed-methods analysis. *LGBT Health, 8*(4), 273–280. https://doi.org/10.1089/lgbt.2020.0437

Virupaksha, H. G., Muralidhar, D., & Ramakrishna, J. (2016a). Suicide and suicidal behavior among transgender persons. *Indian Journal of Psychological Medicine, 38*(6), 505–509. https://doi.org/10.4103/0253-7176.194908

Virupaksha, H. G., Muralidhar, D., & Ramakrishna, J. (2016b). Suicide and suicidal behavior among transgender persons. *Indian Journal of Psychological Medicine, 38*(6), 505–509. https://doi.org/10.4103/0253-7176.194908

Wamsley, L. (2022, October 26). *Most teens who start puberty suppression continue gender-affirming care, study finds.* NPR. https://www.npr.org/2022/10/26/1131398960/gender-affirming-care-trans-puberty-suppression-teens

WANAMAKER, M. H. (2012). Industrialization and fertility in the nineteenth century: Evidence from South Carolina. *The Journal of Economic History, 72*(1), 168–196. https://doi.org/10.1017/s0022050711002476

What is rape and sexual assault? | metropolitan police. (n.d.-b). https://www.met.police.uk/advice/advice-and-information/rsa/rape-and-sexual-assau

lt/what-is-rape-and-sexual-assault/

Williams, R. A. (2006). *Like a loaded weapon: The Rehnquist Court, Indian rights, and the legal history of racism in America.* University of Minnesota Press.